Certified Nurse Educator Exam Practice Questions

CNE® Practice Tests and Review for the Certified Nurse Educator Examination

Written and edited by the Mometrix Test Prep

Printed in the United States of America

This paper meets the requirements of ANSI/NISO Z39.48-1992 (Permanence of Paper).

Paperback
ISBN 13: 978-1-5167-3352-1
ISBN 10: 1-5167-3352-5

Dear Future Exam Success Story

First of all, **THANK YOU** for purchasing Mometrix study materials!

Second, congratulations! You are one of the few determined test-takers who are committed to doing whatever it takes to excel on your exam. **You have come to the right place.** We developed these practice tests with one goal in mind: to deliver you the best possible approximation of the questions you will see on test day.

Standardized testing is one of the biggest obstacles on your road to success, which only increases the importance of doing well in the high-pressure, high-stakes environment of test day. Your results on this test could have a significant impact on your future, and these practice tests will give you the repetitions you need to build your familiarity and confidence with the test content and format to help you achieve your full potential on test day.

Your success is our success

We would love to hear from you! If you would like to share the story of your exam success or if you have any questions or comments in regard to our products, please contact us at **800-673-8175** or **support@mometrix.com**.

Thanks again for your business and we wish you continued success!

Sincerely,
The Mometrix Test Preparation Team

Written and edited by the Mometrix Exam Secrets Test Prep Team
Printed in the United States of America

Table of Contents

Nurse Educator Practice Test #1

1. Which of the following is a major obstacle to patient learning?

a. Early discharge
b. Third-party reimbursement
c. Concerns regarding patient coercion
d. Lack of self-confidence

2. Which one of the following students would be classified as a traditional undergraduate nursing student?

a. A 26-year-old female
b. A 24-year-old male
c. A 20-year-old student speaking English as a second language
d. A 23-year-old female residing in off-campus housing

3. The school of nursing does not require that nurse educators serve on academic committees during the year of hire but strongly encourages participation and considers committee work during evaluation. In the first year of hire, how many committees should the nurse educator ideally volunteer to serve on?

a. None
b. One
c. Two to three
d. Three or more

4. The nurse educator believes that the education in orthopedics needs to focus more on rehabilitation and wants to revise the curriculum to include clinical experience in a rehabilitation facility. The nurse should initially discuss this with whom?

a. The academic dean
b. The vice president of health
c. The chair of the nursing department
d. Other nurse educators

5. Online classes are most suitable for which type of student?

a. Self-motivated
b. Mature adult
c. Employed
d. Young

6. Considering elements of the nurse evaluation, which of the following is considered an element of professional service?

a. Teaching classes
b. Publishing an article in a nursing journal
c. Serving on the board of a national nursing organization
d. Making a presentation at a state nursing conference

7. When designing curriculum for a class, which of the following is the most important element to consider?

a. The students
b. The costs
c. The faculty
d. The time frame

8. As a social networking tool, which of the following social media sites is most appropriate for a nursing professional?

a. Snapchat
b. Facebook
c. Instagram
d. LinkedIn

9. A nurse educator is concerned that students have been cheating on exams and is about to administer a multiple-choice exam. Which of the following is the best method to prevent cheating?

a. Warn the students of the consequences of cheating.
b. Place the same questions but in random order on each exam.
c. Place the students two seats apart from each other.
d. Give each student a separate exam with different questions.

10. A nurse educator notes that two students have 16 errors in common on a 100-item multiple-choice test, but in the rest of the class, students ranged from four to eight errors in common. Because the nurse educator suspects that the students have cheated, the best initial approach is to take which of the following actions?

a. Provide the statistical evidence.
b. Tell the students they were observed cheating.
c. Ask the students if they cheated.
d. Require the students to retake the test.

11. A nurse educator has been assigned to teach a new subject. Which of the following steps should the nurse educator do first?

a. Research the subject.
b. Assess personal knowledge and expertise in the subject.
c. Review similar classes.
d. Consider innovative teaching methods.

12. The nurse educator shows a group of nursing students a film that demonstrates how to do a procedure. After the viewing, most students are able to explain the steps, but two students seem very confused. Which teaching intervention may be most helpful?

a. Show the students the film again.
b. Give the students an audiotape describing the procedure.
c. Provide a diagram showing the procedure.
d. Allow the students to have hands-on practice.

13. A review of National Council Licensure Examination (NCLEX) passing rates on the first attempt shows that over the previous 10 years, the passing rate has decreased from 90% to 76%. Most current students are in their twenties. Which of the following initial steps is most indicated?

a. Assess teaching strategies.
b. Increase entrance requirements.
c. Modify curriculum.
d. Admit older students.

14. Which of the following is the most valuable initial strategy to use with a group of 10 new nursing students meeting in a class with the instructor for the first time?

a. Introduction activity (student-focused)
b. Outline of course content
c. Description of class rules
d. Explanation of grading policies

15. The nurse educator assigned groups of new students to discuss the reasons for becoming a nurse. Although most groups provided serious reasons, one group developed a list of satirical reasons, including "Marry a rich doctor" and "Easy access to drugs." Which of the following is the best response by the nurse educator?

a. Give the students a low grade.
b. Chastise the students for not taking the assignment seriously.
c. Use the students' list as the basis for a discussion.
d. Meet individually with the students to determine their motivation.

16. Which of the following learning theories is a nurse educator using when she gives rewards to students who complete all assignments on time?

a. Behaviorism
b. Cognitivism
c. Constructivism
d. Humanism

17. According to Gagne's nine events of instruction, which of the following instructional events comes first?

a. Inform students of objectives.
b. Stimulate recall.
c. Provide feedback.
d. Gain students' attention.

18. According to the theory of deep learning, which of the following is an example of surface learning?

a. Doing everything necessary to study the material
b. Memorizing facts, figures, and details
c. Relating current material to previously learned material
d. Attempting to understand the concepts behind information

19. According to Keller's ARCS model of motivating students, the letter "R" stands for which of the following?

a. Reeducation
b. Relevance
c. References
d. Reevaluation

20. Which of the following change theories considers that three essential elements are the individual person, the environment, and personal factors (behavior, cognition) and that changing one will change the others?

a. Behavior modification theory
b. Theory of planned behavior
c. Social cognitive theory
d. Social learning theory

21. According to Van Manen's theory of pedagogy, the basis of teaching is what relationship?

a. Sibling
b. Master/servant
c. Parent/child
d. Peer

22. Which of the following is a characteristic of andragogy?

a. Students may gain insight from life experiences.
b. Students have few responsibilities.
c. Students may not understand the long-term need for study material.
d. Students often do not retain the study material.

23. A nurse supervisor comments that she has two male nursing students on her unit and that she doesn't feel comfortable having them assigned to female patients. This is primarily an example of which of the following?

a. Discrimination
b. Poor judgment
c. Stereotyping
d. Bias

24. The nurse educator describes a personal experience as a nursing student to describe a nursing concept and asks the students to do further research on the subject and report back to the class. According to Quirk's classification, which teaching style is the nurse educator using for this lesson?

a. Facilitative
b. Suggestive
c. Assertive
d. Collaborative

25. The nurse educator assesses the students with the Kolb learning style inventory. Based on this inventory, students who are classified as accommodative will likely do best with which type of learning experience?

a. Active practice and experimentation
b. Time for reflection
c. Presentation of abstract concepts
d. Passive observation

26. A colleague tells a newly hired nurse educator, "The suggestions you made were a complete waste of time, and if you want to get along with the staff, you need to stop trying to make changes." This is an example of which of the following?

a. Discrimination
b. Advice
c. Vertical violence
d. Horizontal/lateral violence

27. Which of the following is the correct wording of a learning objective?

a. "The nursing student will be able to accurately determine intravenous drop rates."
b. "By the end of the training module, the nursing student will demonstrate correct administration of insulin."
c. "At some point in the semester, the nursing student will demonstrate knowledge of effective wound care."
d. "By the end of the training session, the nursing student will demonstrate correct handwashing techniques in all clinical and instructional settings 100% of the time."

28. The nurse educator is developing a lesson plan for teaching nursing students about diabetic ketoacidosis. The most important goal of a lesson plan is to do which of the following?

a. Make sure students meet educational goals.
b. Prepare students for taking the NCLEX exam.
c. Provide a record of class instruction.
d. Communicate with other faculty.

29. The nurse educator has been using a collaborative learning approach, assigning groups of students to work on projects together, but it has become clear that some students are contributing little to the groups, causing resentment among those students who are contributing. Which of the following is the best approach to solving this problem?

a. Stop assigning group projects.
b. Give students a group grade and an individual grade.
c. Give noncontributing students a lower grade than other group members.
d. Remind the students that all must contribute to group projects.

30. A nurse educator conducted a discussion about a case study with a group of 10 students, but one student dominated the discussion and one student failed to contribute at all. Which of the following is the best solution?

a. Remind students that they all need to contribute equally to discussions.
b. Guide the discussion by calling on students at random, ensuring that all participate.
c. Continue with the same procedures, recognizing that students participate differently.
d. Ask the student who dominated to allow others more time to contribute.

31. The nurse educator for psychiatric nursing has asked the students to do reflective journaling as part of the clinical experience, assuring the students that only the nurse educator will read the journals. One student writes in her journal that she has been struggling with drug addiction and is sometimes using cocaine. Which initial step by the nurse educator is most indicated?

a. Discuss the issue with the head of the department.
b. Inform the student that she will be expelled from nursing school.
c. Meet with the student to discuss the issue.
d. Discuss the issue with the school nurse/physician.

32. The nursing students are preparing to work with hospice patients and are unsure how to respond to patients. Which of the following teaching strategies may be most effective in helping students respond appropriately?

a. Group discussion
b. Humor
c. One-on-one instruction
d. Role-playing

33. As part of clinical training, small groups of students use a lifelike simulator to practice responding to a series of increasingly serious postoperative complications. One group becomes completely dysfunctional and is unable to respond adequately to any of the simulated complications. The best response of the nurse educator is to say which of the following?

a. "You just killed your patient!"
b. "You need to do that simulation again."
c. "Let's talk about where things went wrong."
d. "Why didn't you follow your nursing procedures?"

34. The nurse educator is using computer-assisted instruction and designing a module about nursing ethics. Which of the following is the most important consideration?

a. Font size
b. Layout
c. Color scheme
d. Interactivity

35. The nurse educator shares information about educational grants with the students, encourages them to discuss their clinical observations, and urges them to present case studies at an upcoming conference and to begin networking. These are examples of which of the following?

a. Supervising
b. Role-modeling
c. Mentoring
d. Teaching

36. The nurse educator is developing a slide show for an upcoming discussion with a group of students about learning styles. Which of the following is the best format?

a. Detailed explanations in narrative format
b. Limiting words to 200 per slide
c. Use of multiple styles and colors of fonts
d. Limited explanations and bulleted lists

37. Which of the following is the best use of video podcasting (vodcasting)?

a. Providing assignments
b. Recording lectures
c. Supervising students
d. Evaluating students

38. The nurse educator has designed an exercise in critical thinking. The students are asked to identify solution-focused responses and cause-focused responses to a patient who repeatedly complains of unrelieved postoperative pain on the third postoperative day. Which of the following is a cause-focused response?

a. Give pain medication per patient request.
b. Ask the physician for a prescription for a stronger medication.
c. Advise the patient to practice visualization and relaxation exercises.
d. Examine wound for signs of infection.

39. The nurse educator tells the students that they must be able to demonstrate skills prior to performing them. This is an example of which of the following?

a. Evidence-based education
b. Modeling
c. Mentoring
d. Skill-focused education

40. Which teaching strategies are likely to be most effective for visual learners?

a. Podcasts
b. Slide show presentations
c. Simulations
d. Lectures

41. The nurse educator has several international students who seemed to be doing well in class and did well on an essay exam but did very poorly on the final multiple-choice test. Which initial strategy is most likely to be effective?

a. Arrange tutoring for the students.
b. Provide one-on-one instruction.
c. Give a workshop on test-taking.
d. Pair international students with native students for studying.

42. A nursing student complains to the nurse educator that a fellow student from the Middle East is behaving inappropriately. When questioned more closely, the student states that the Middle Eastern student stands very close to her when they talk and breathes on her. Which response is most appropriate?

a. Counsel the Middle Eastern student to avoid standing so close to others.
b. Counsel the nursing student who is complaining to try to be more tolerant.
c. Conduct a class lesson regarding proxemics and cultural differences.
d. Conduct a class lesson about tolerance for other cultures.

43. The nursing school has developed a program for disadvantaged students to attend. The nurse educator finds the students motivated but doing poorly in class because they lack the necessary academic skills. Which intervention is likely to be most effective?

a. Establish a study support group.
b. Advise the students to work on study skills.
c. Place the students on academic probation.
d. Discuss study skills with the entire class.

44. Which of the following most accurately describes a course syllabus?

a. A general class outline with assignments
b. An explanation of the teaching strategies and materials used for the class
c. A complete description of the class and assignments
d. A legal contract outlining the course content and responsibilities of the instructor and the students

45. A nurse educator develops a course syllabus, reviews it with the students, and posts it online, but two weeks later feels that the grading criteria are lenient and wants to make a change. Which of the following options is available to the nurse educator?

a. The nurse educator may access the document and change the grading criteria.
b. The nurse educator may not make changes to the grading criteria until the current academic session ends.
c. The nurse educator may tell the students verbally that the grading criteria have changed.
d. The nurse educator may request that the academic dean approve changing the grading criteria.

46. When developing a course and writing behavioral objectives, which of the following is a general example of psychomotor objectives?

a. Tasks and specific skills
b. Values and beliefs
c. Empirical knowledge/information
d. Feelings

47. The nurse educator is writing course objectives using Bloom's original taxonomy (1956) as a guide and focusing on cognitive learning. One objective directs the student to explain a concept. To which domain does the objective apply?

a. Knowledge
b. Comprehension
c. Evaluation
d. Synthesis

48. A new nurse educator is planning a course for the first time. Which of the following is likely to be the biggest challenge?

a. Course content
b. Evaluation
c. Time allocation
d. Teaching strategies

49. When planning teaching strategies and classroom activities, the nurse educator keeps in mind that the average adult attention span is how long?

a. 5–10 minutes
b. 10–15 minutes
c. 15–20 minutes
d. 20–30 minutes

50. The nurse educator is scheduled to teach a lesson about hospice care, with which she has had little experience. Which of the following is probably the best solution?

a. Research hospice care to prepare for the lesson.
b. Assign the students to research hospice care and present their findings.
c. Ask other faculty for advice about teaching the lesson.
d. Arrange for a hospice nurse to be a guest speaker.

51. The nurse educator is collaborating with community organizations to place nursing students so they can observe and gain knowledge of community health needs. Which is likely to be the best organization in which to place students?

a. Free clinic serving homeless and low-income community members
b. Meals On Wheels home meal delivery program
c. Public health vaccination clinic
d. Breast-cancer screening agency

52. The nurse educator is evaluating textbooks and reading assignments for a class. In general, how many pages per week of reading should the instructor expect students to be able to manage in an upper division class?

a. 50 to 75
b. 75 to 100
c. 100 to 150
d. 200 to 300

53. The school of nursing uses a course management system that includes course rosters, grade books, course syllabi, classroom discussions, course content and materials, messaging, and space to upload assignments. What is the primary advantage of this type of system?

a. Cost saving
b. Ease of access
c. Time saving
d. Student compliance

54. The nurse educator wishes to conduct an item analysis to establish the reliability of testing. Which type of exam will best facilitate this research?

a. Multiple-choice exam
b. True/false exam
c. Mixed-format exam
d. Electronic or computerized exam

55. A nurse educator has been charged with developing an online course for nursing ethics. Which of the following is the best preparation for developing an online course?

a. Research online courses.
b. Discuss online courses with experienced instructors.
c. Get a "how-to" manual.
d. Take an online course.

56. When teaching abstract concepts to students, which of the following is the most effective teaching strategy?

a. Use real-life, concrete examples.
b. Go slow and repeat often.
c. Ask for student feedback.
d. Test students for comprehension.

57. The nurse educator is scheduled to teach three classes. What is the most important for the nurse educator to know?

a. The school's philosophy
b. The students
c. Various teaching strategies
d. The course content

58. The nurse educator has been asked to serve on a committee to redesign courses to include problem-based learning. What initial action is indicated?

a. Visit programs that use problem-based learning.
b. Review literature about problem-based learning.
c. Ask for faculty input.
d. Solicit volunteers to use problem-based learning on a trial basis.

59. The nurse educator is setting up stations for assessment of clinical skills using objective structured clinical evaluation (OSCE). Which of the following is a critical element to consider?

a. The stations should be individualized for the students.
b. All students should have the same experience and receive the same questions.
c. Students should be allowed as much time as needed at each station.
d. Students should receive immediate feedback at each station.

60. Admission to the school of nursing requires that students complete an anatomy and physiology course with a grade of A or B, and the course may only be repeated one time to improve a lower grade; however, many students are unable to get an A or B in two attempts. Which of the following is the best solution?

a. Lower the required grade to C.
b. Allow students to repeat the course three times.
c. Establish a tutoring program to assist students in the course.
d. Take no action.

61. Formative evaluations are usually used to do which of the following?

a. Assess the effectiveness of teaching during a course.
b. Assign class grades.
c. Assess student competencies at the end of a course.
d. Revise curriculum.

62. According to Dave's taxonomy for development of psychomotor skills, which step must the student do first?

a. Manipulation
b. Precision
c. Articulation
d. Imitation

63. The nurse educator routinely assigns the "one-minute paper" at the end of each classroom session. The primary purpose is to do which of the following?

a. Assess the effectiveness of the class.
b. Assess the students' ability to write.
c. Assess the students' knowledge.
d. Assess the nurse educator.

64. The "three R's" of mentoring are reflecting, reframing, and which of the following?

a. Recalling
b. Reevaluating
c. Resolving
d. Reciprocating

65. The school of nursing is incorporating Writing Across the Curriculum into all coursework. Students will be expected to write in a variety of different formats, including essays, narrative reports, summaries, and case studies. What is the best strategy for helping students to write successfully?

a. Provide clear directions and writing samples for all writing assignments.
b. Require a writing course specifically for nursing students.
c. Require students to pass a writing competency test before admission to nursing school.
d. Provide a writing workshop for instructors.

66. Which type of validity considers the effect that the environment of testing has on the student's behavior?

a. Criterion validity
b. Ecological validity
c. Face validity
d. Construct validity

67. The nurse educator administers a final exam and asks the students to evaluate whether the test covered the material in a fair and consistent manner. The students responded 96% positively and 4% negatively. The nurse educator can conclude that the test has which type of validity?

a. Content validity
b. Criterion validity
c. Construct validity
d. Face validity

68. The nurse educator is conducting a hierarchical task analysis of clinical skills. Which of the following is the first task when conducting hierarchical task analysis?

a. Select and group tasks.
b. Organize tasks within groups.
c. Regroup.
d. Seek expert advice if necessary.

69. What is the first level of Krathwhol's affective taxonomy?

a. Responding
b. Organization
c. Receiving
d. Characterization by value or value complex

70. As part of student evaluations, the nurse educator is planning to include an authentic assessment. Which of the following would be appropriate?

a. An essay exam
b. A simulation exercise
c. A student demonstration
d. A student debate of moral issues

71. The nurse educator is designing clinical evaluation tools to be used by all instructors during the clinical evaluations of a cohort of students at the end of the semester. Which of the following methods is most likely to ensure inter-instructor reliability?

a. Careful assessment of content validity
b. Multiple instructors assessing the same group of students and comparing results
c. Multiple instructors assessing the same student and comparing results
d. A single instructor assessing a group of students and others using the results as a basis for scoring

72. The nurse educator is planning the clinical rotation for a student in a wheelchair. Which of the following should be an initial concern?

a. Determining which accommodations are necessary
b. Ensuring staff support
c. Limiting the student's caseload
d. Assigning another student to assist the wheelchair-bound student

73. The nurse educator has completed a curriculum design process that will bring about several changes in the nursing education program. Which of the following is the best initial step to ensure acceptance?

a. Educating the staff about the changes they must incorporate
b. Instituting a pilot program on a small scale
c. Asking for faculty opinions about proposed changes
d. Reminding faculty members that changes were mandated by administration

74. The nurse educator is planning faculty development activities to encourage staff members to take an active role in curriculum development. Which of the following should be the initial focus of the activities?

a. Curriculum design
b. Evaluation formats
c. Identification of outcomes
d. Leadership

75. The nurse educator is to be part of a committee charged with redesigning the curriculum to focus more on learner outcomes. Before initiating curriculum development activities, the committee should do which of the following?

a. Decide whom to include in the process.
b. Determine the structure of the committee.
c. Select a change theory to serve as a guide.
d. Decide on a system of communication.

76. The nurse is serving on the curriculum design committee and considering ways to encourage more staff support and participation. The best solution is to do which of the following?

a. Submit weekly update reports to other staff.
b. Conduct staff meetings to explain the committee's goals.
c. Ask administration to give a directive to staff.
d. Establish several ad hoc committees comprised of staff members.

77. When gathering data about internal contextual factors as part of curriculum development, what data collecting method would be appropriate to gain information about organizational culture?

a. Survey
b. Review of documents and interviews
c. Observation
d. Focus group

78. As part of curriculum design, the nurse educator wants to include more simulations using high-tech mannequins, but the administration is not willing to provide financial resources. The nurse educator's initial strategy should be to do which of the following?

a. Plan alternate teaching methods.
b. Make another appeal to administration.
c. Research available grants.
d. Conduct fund-raising activities.

79. The nurse educator is teaching critical thinking skills to new nursing students and wants to evaluate the effectiveness of the teaching strategies used during the course. Which of the following may provide the best information?

a. Pre- and posttests
b. Student surveys
c. Observations
d. Nursing staff surveys

80. When conducting program assessment, the nurse educator notes that the highest dropout rate for male and female nursing students occurs during the obstetrics and gynecology (OB-GYN) clinical rotation. Which of the following actions is indicated initially?

a. Interview clinical supervisors.
b. Advise faculty to give extra support to students during the OB-GYN rotation.
c. Conduct a learner needs evaluation.
d. Advise faculty to use different teaching strategies.

81. When conducting a program assessment, the primary advantage to using an internal evaluator is which of the following?

a. The evaluator is more likely to be objective.
b. The evaluator has a better overall understanding of the program.
c. The evaluator does not incur extra costs to the program.
d. The evaluator increases the credibility of the assessment.

82. The nurse educator is assigned to a curriculum redesign committee to change the program to one that is competency-based and focused on learner outcomes. To obtain input regarding necessary competencies, which of the following initial strategies may provide the best information?

a. Student surveys
b. Observation
c. Research into best practices
d. Focus groups

83. Which of the following evaluation models focuses on evidence-based evaluation and continuous self-evaluation to determine if outcomes are being met?

a. Decision-oriented model
b. Fourth-generation model
c. Logic/reason model
d. Accreditation model

84. As part of program assessment, the nurse educator is reviewing the reliability coefficient of four achievement tests:

Test 1: 0.86
Test 2: 0.74
Test 3: 0.50
Test 4: 0.60

Which test is generally reliable but will require revision of a few items?

a. Test 1
b. Test 2
c. Test 3
d. Test 4

85. When evaluating students, the nurse educator includes the following: "Calculate the drip rate needed to deliver 500 mL of NS in 4 hours with a drop factor of 15 drops per mL." This type of examination question is focused on which of the following?

a. Application
b. Evaluation
c. Synthesis
d. Analysis

86. A student with dyslexia reads slowly and often is unable to finish written exams but does extremely well on clinical demonstrations and answers questions well verbally. Which one of the following accommodations is most indicated?

a. None, all students must have equal testing.
b. Substitute oral exams for written.
c. Allow the student extra time for test taking.
d. Provide one-on-one instruction in test-taking strategies.

87. A Muslim student has applied to the school of nursing, indicating that she is observant and wears the hijab and keeps her arms and legs covered even though institutional policy requires that students and staff have arms exposed below the elbow and the head uncovered. Which of the following is the best solution?

a. Notify the student that she cannot be admitted to the school.
b. Allow the student to ignore the policies if admitted.
c. Meet with the infection control officer to develop policies for observant Muslim students.
d. Ask the student to consider following institutional policies if admitted.

88. The nurse educator has been asked to chair a committee but is concerned that he lacks adequate leadership experience. The nurse educator's initial action should be to do which of the following?

a. Turn down the request until he gains more experience.
b. Take a continuing education course on leadership.
c. Ask others for advice about leadership.
d. Assess his own leadership style and skills.

89. The nurse educator is chairing a curriculum design committee, and one committee member is very negative, constantly complaining and disagreeing with everyone's suggestions but contributing little. During one discussion, the member states, "Your ideas are stupid." What is the best response?

a. "Please keep your comments civil."
b. "Your comments are not appropriate."
c. "If you are really unhappy with the group's ideas, perhaps you should consider working on a different committee."
d. "We'd like to hear your ideas. What do you suggest?"

90. The nurse educator is in the first year working in the faculty of a school of nursing and is considering career goals for the first year. Realistically, how many career goal activities should the nurse educator try to accomplish in the first year beyond those expected as part of her role as an educator?

a. One or two
b. As many as possible
c. None
d. Three to five

91. The first step to networking is to do which of the following?

a. Meet and get to know as many staff members as possible.
b. Join local, state, and national organizations.
c. Inventory personal and professional connections.
d. Ask for the advice of more experienced staff.

92. The nurse educator is newly graduated and has been offered positions at an associate degree and a baccalaureate degree program. Which is the best position for him to accept?

a. The associate degree program
b. The baccalaureate degree program
c. Either, because the choice is not an important consideration
d. Either, depending on career goals

93. Which element of malpractice is involved if a nurse fails to provide a patient with care consistent with basic standards of care for the patient's condition?

a. Duty to client
b. Breach of duty
c. Causation
d. Damage

94. The institution has been found negligent by vicarious liability because of the actions of a nurse employee. The principle of indemnification allows the institution to do which of the following?

a. Avoid paying a penalty.
b. Sue the negligent nurse to regain money paid as damages.
c. Shield the negligent nurse from any liability.
d. Withhold salary from the negligent nurse to pay damages.

95. A nursing student performed cardiopulmonary resuscitation (CPR) on an elderly patient, who was successfully resuscitated but suffered fractured ribs because of external compressions. Which ethical principle did the student violate to save the patient's life?

a. Beneficence
b. Autonomy
c. Justice
d. Nonmaleficence

96. The nurse educator is considering long- and short-term professional goals using the SMART guidelines (Drucker), which state that goals should be specific, measurable, attainable, realistic, and which of the following?

a. Targeted
b. Transferrable
c. Time-oriented
d. Tangible

97. The nurse educator is reviewing test questions to determine if they are discriminating. If they are, the nurse educator expects which of the following to be true?

a. The upper third of the students will answer the questions correctly.
b. The upper third of the students will not answer the questions correctly.
c. The lower third of the students will answer the questions correctly.
d. The middle third of the students will not answer the questions correctly.

98. Which of the following is most likely to increase the nurse's socialization to the role of nurse educator?

a. Conference attendance
b. Organization membership
c. Participation in academic committees
d. Mentoring

99. The most important commitment to education for the nurse educator is to do which of the following?

a. Take continuing education courses.
b. Engage in lifelong learning.
c. Increase knowledge in the area of expertise.
d. Meet certification requirements.

100. The primary function of a nurse leader is to do which of the following?

a. Serve as a role model.
b. Make decisions.
c. Collaborate.
d. Effect change.

101. When using Lewin's force field analysis to help facilitate a change, the nurse educator must first consider which of the following?

a. Financial costs
b. Administrative support
c. Driving and restraining forces
d. Organizational culture

102. The most important manner by which the nurse educator is expected to show cultural competence is through which of the following actions?

a. Demonstrating respect for those with different values and cultures
b. Completing coursework related to cultural diversity
c. Establishing relationships with those of other cultures
d. Demonstrating knowledge of other cultures

103. Which of the following shows recognition of a nurse educator's scholarship?

a. Receiving a scheduled raise in salary
b. Being assigned to a committee
c. Receiving a grant
d. Serving on a hiring board

104. The nurse educator telephones a legislator to speak in favor of a law that allows nurses increased autonomy. This is primarily an example of which of the following?

a. Networking
b. Advocacy
c. Leadership
d. Collaboration

105. The primary purpose of the American Nurses Advocacy Institute is to do which of the following?

a. Advocate for patients' right to make end-of-life decisions.
b. Promote the career of nursing.
c. Train nurses as patient advocates.
d. Train nurses to become political leaders.

106. Based on provisions of the Affordable Care Act, the nurse educator believes that nursing education needs a larger focus on which of the following?

a. Prevention
b. Postsurgical care
c. Cardiac care
d. Rehabilitation

107. The model of program assessment that focuses on the way things are done rather than the outcomes is which of the following?

a. Goal model
b. Systems model
c. Process model
d. Competing values framework

108. The nurse educator is using Rogers' diffusion of innovation theory to gain acceptance for an innovation in clinical education for students. Which stage of acceptance must the nurse attend to first?

a. Communication
b. Persuasion
c. Confirmation
d. Knowledge

109. The nurse educator is providing training to student nurses to prepare them to do peer evaluations using a standardized form. The nurse educator stresses that the most important element of the peer evaluation is to do which of the following?

a. Fully complete the form.
b. Provide concrete examples to support scoring.
c. Complete it in a timely manner.
d. Provide feedback during the evaluation.

110. When conducting research, which database is most appropriate for the nurse educator to access to obtain full-text nursing and health journals?

a. PubMed
b. Cochrane
c. CINAHL
d. Medline

111. Three nurse educators are teaching different sections of the same course and have agreed on four student learning outcomes. Which of the following is the most important factor to ensure adequate assessment?

a. Same course assignments and content
b. Same outcomes assessment tool and scoring criteria
c. Same grading standards
d. Same method of teaching to the learning outcomes

112. Which of the following is the best use of student learning outcomes data?

a. Assess the overall effectiveness of the curricula.
b. Assess individual departments.
c. Use data as part of faculty evaluation.
d. Rank faculty.

113. Which of the following assignments is likely the MOST effective method of improving students' leadership skills?

a. Assigning groups of students to research and lead class discussions on both sides of sociocultural issues
b. Assigning students to write an essay about leadership
c. Conducting a leadership skills assessment
d. Leading a discussion about "What is a leader?"

114. A nurse educator asks a more experienced educator for assistance in improving teaching skills. Which of the following is the best first step?

a. The experienced educator provides a written list of teaching strategies.
b. The newly hired nurse educator gives a teaching demonstration to the experienced educator.
c. The experienced educator observes the nurse educator teaching a class.
d. The nurse educator observes the experienced educator teaching a class.

115. The nurse educator is working with students on a research project regarding different approaches to care. Which type of validity is supported when research findings can be generalized to other populations beyond those in the research project?

a. Internal
b. Construct
c. External
d. Face

116. The nurse educator is teaching research design to a group of students. Which of the following should the nurse educator stress as the most effective method of controlling the intrinsic factors related to research subjects?

a. Matching
b. Randomization
c. Homogeneity
d. Blocking

117. The nurse educator is an instructor in an associate degree program at a small community college, and the state has cut funding to the college by $2.5 million dollars, a move that will impact all programs. Which of the following should be the nurse educator's highest priority?

a. Identifying cost-cutting measures
b. Justifying budgetary expenses
c. Garnering support for the nursing program among other departments
d. Stressing the importance of the program to the local community

118. The nurse educator is part of a committee evaluating the nursing program and assessing the need for change. Which of the following should be the primary focus when instituting change?

a. Current trends in higher education
b. Staff preference
c. Community needs
d. Best available evidence-based research

119. Which of the following is the best example of an observational learning experience for students?

a. Assisting in surgery
b. Watching an autopsy
c. Watching a physician debride a patient's wound
d. Caring for a patient under direct supervision

120. The nursing program has established a classroom to clinical hours ratio of 1:3. If a student is in class eight hours per week, how many clinical hours should he be assigned to each week?

a. 4
b. 8
c. 12
d. 24

121. According to the Institute of Medicine (IOM), what percentage of the complete nursing workforce was hoped to have obtained at least a baccalaureate degree in nursing by the year 2020?

a. 25%
b. 50%
c. 80%
d. 100%

122. The nurse educator is planning a simulation exercise, using student actors from an acting class on campus as well as students in allied health fields. Which of the following exercises is the best to help nursing students address the Quality and Safety Education for Nurses (QSEN) competency of interdisciplinary collaboration and teamwork?

a. Assisting to evacuate mothers and infants from obstetrics because of toxic fumes
b. Assisting with triage at a school after an earthquake caused the building to collapse, injuring many faculty and students
c. Assisting nurses working with indigent patients in a free clinic
d. Assisting in the transfer of patients from an Alzheimer's unit to another unit after a small fire has caused smoke damage

123. According to the nurse educator's grading policy for papers, the student loses a letter grade for each 24 hours the paper is submitted after the due date and time. One student has repeatedly turned in late papers, despite the nurse educator's offers of one-on-one assistance and counseling of the student. Because of the late papers, the student is failing the class. What is the most appropriate action?

a. Meet with the student and arrange for the student to make up work.
b. Fail the student.
c. Give the student the grades she would have earned if the papers were on time.
d. Give the student an "incomplete" grade in the class, and allow her to redo the late papers.

124. Which of the following actions by a student supports the Joint Commission's goal to reduce the risk of healthcare-associated infection?

a. The student uses an alcohol-based skin cleanser to wash blood from his hands after caring for a patient.
b. The student places the patient's dirty linen on the floor.
c. The student moves the patient's urinal to the side of the overbed table to make room for the meal tray.
d. The student wears gloves when helping a patient use a bedpan.

125. Which of the following is the best assignment to help students to use evidence-based practice to improve clinical safety?

a. Ask students to observe and identify a safety issue in clinical practice and then research evidence-based practices regarding the issue.
b. Ask students to read an article about clinical safety and evidence-based practices.
c. Show the students a video about clinical safety and evidence-based practices.
d. Lead a class discussion about clinical safety and evidence-based practices.

126. When the nurse educator is leading a discussion about cause and effect, which type of diagram or chart is most effective?

a. Scattergram
b. Flowchart
c. Ishikawa "fishbone" diagram
d. Pareto chart

127. The nurse educator is teaching a beginning course for student nurses in a registered nurse program. About half of the students have had previous healthcare experience as nurse aides or licensed vocation/practical nurses, and the other half have no experience. Which is the best way to manage these differences?

a. Do not differentiate in any way.
b. Encourage those with healthcare background to share experiences during discussions.
c. Provide added support for those without experience.
d. Provide more difficult class assignments for those with healthcare experience.

128. Which of the following is an extrinsic motivator for an adult learner?

a. Enjoyment
b. Job satisfaction
c. Self-esteem
d. Certificate of achievement

129. The nurse educator is writing a competency statement for program evaluation. Which of the following competency statements is the most appropriate?

a. "Uses a variety of different feedback and outcomes data to evaluate the effectiveness of the program"
b. "Follows industry standards in evaluating the program"
c. "Evaluates program fairly using various measures"
d. "Uses subjective and objective information to evaluate the program effectiveness"

130. The nurse educator is the chair of the committee planning staff education programs. Which of the following should the committee do first?

a. Identify goals.
b. Plan assessment measures.
c. Conduct a needs assessment.
d. Determine cost-effectiveness.

131. The nurse educator has presented a staff education program. Which of the following shows that operational integration has been achieved?

a. Staff members demonstrate learning during assessment.
b. Staff members express satisfaction with the program.
c. Course objectives are met.
d. Staff members exhibit behavioral changes.

132. The nurse educator is using a textbook that has ancillary electronic study materials available, but few students are accessing the material. What is the best approach for the nurse educator?

a. Conduct a class orientation to show them how to access and use the material.
b. Advise the class that the ancillary material is helpful.
c. Include the ancillary material in class assignments.
d. Discontinue use of the ancillary study material.

133. The nurse educator is planning to shift the focus in a course from teacher-centered to learner-centered. Which of the following is the best reason for this change?

a. Students usually prefer learner-centered approaches.
b. The instructor's role is minimized.
c. Students are likely to retain the information better.
d. Class assignments require less time to plan.

134. Which of the following is an example of an unstructured learning activity as part of inquiry-based learning?

a. The student summarizes an article and gives a class presentation.
b. The student researches a subject and leads a class discussion.
c. The student participates in a simulation exercise.
d. The student attends an Alcoholics Anonymous (AA) meeting.

135. Which of the following student learning activities is most effective to develop the affective domain?

a. Presenting a case study related to teaching a patient and his family about disease prevention
b. Preparing a summary of an article about different methods of birth control
c. Giving a slide show presentation about chemotherapy
d. Demonstrating a colostomy irrigation

136. At the most basic level, instruction regarding informatics should prepare the student to do which of the following?

a. Use a computer.
b. Access databases and research patient care issues.
c. Develop evidence-based practices.
d. Prepare electronic presentations.

137. According to the nurse educator transition (NET) model for nurses making the transition from clinical nursing to educating, which stage is the nurse educator in when beginning teaching?

a. Anticipation
b. Information-seeking
c. Disorientation
d. Formation of identity

138. Which of the following is the greatest concern related to the shortage of nurse educators in nursing faculties?

a. Salaries
b. Education
c. Time constraints
d. Age of current nurse educators

139. The nurse educator is responsible for evaluating the skills of a group of nursing students. Which of the following is most important?

a. Making unannounced observations
b. Documenting all observations and findings
c. Including subjective evaluation
d. Considering observations of clinical staff

140. Which of the following is the primary reason that nursing programs are accepting limited numbers of applicants?

a. Lack of financial support
b. Lack of administrative support
c. Lack of faculty
d. Lack of prepared students

141. Which of the following is the final and most critical step in a cycle of action research?

a. Planning
b. Acting
c. Observing
d. Reflecting

142. The nurse educator is planning a lesson on the peripheral nervous system and reflex arcs. Which teaching strategy is most likely to ensure that the information received in short-term memory becomes encoded into long-term memory?

a. Lecture
b. Commercial video presentation
c. Student-created video presentation
d. Class discussion

143. Which type of memory allows students to carry out actions automatically, without conscious thought?

a. Explicit
b. Autobiographical
c. Short-term
d. Implicit

144. Which philosophy of evaluation orientation focuses on identifying student strengths and weaknesses?

a. Service
b. Practice
c. Judgmental
d. Constructivist

145. The nurse educator is conducting item analysis and wants to identify the median score on an exam with 50 questions (2 points per question). The students received the following scores:

100	86
94	84, 84 (2 students)
92	78
90	72
88	34

Which is the median score?

a. 81
b. 84
c. 86
d. 88

146. The student evaluations indicate that students feel that the nurse educator grades essays unfairly and inconsistently. What is the most appropriate response?

a. Ignore the evaluations.
b. Establish a grading rubric to follow.
c. Ask the students for advice about grading.
d. Attempt to justify grading.

147. Which of the following is an example of emotional intelligence?

a. Smiling and being nice to people at all times
b. Freely expressing all emotions in all situations
c. Understanding but suppressing emotions in all situations
d. Understanding and perceiving emotions in self and others

148. The nurse educator is evaluating textbooks for reading ease using the Flesch–Kincaid scale and wants to select a textbook that is difficult but appropriate for freshman college students. Which average sentence length (in words) is appropriate for college-level textbooks?

a. 30
b. 14
c. 25
d. 11

149. Which demographic trend is likely to have the most impact on nursing education?

a. Increased numbers of ethnic minorities
b. Shift in populations from rural areas to urban
c. Increased numbers of women in the workplace
d. Aging of the population

150. The nurse educator should stress to nursing students that the most important focus of patient education is which of the following?

a. Self-care
b. Self-confidence
c. Cost-effectiveness
d. Treatment compliance

Answers and Explanations

1. A: Early discharge is a major obstacle to patient learning. Many procedures are now done on an outpatient basis with minimal preparation (often only printed sheets of information) provided to the patient prior to the procedure. Patients are often discharged within hours, leaving almost no time for instruction. Patients, even those with serious injuries or illnesses, are routinely discharged from acute hospitals to subacute facilities or home within days, so there is little continuity of care or opportunity for patient education.

2. D: A 23-year-old female residing in on- or off-campus housing would be considered a traditional undergraduate nursing student. Those classified as nontraditional (a growing percentage of students) include those 25 years of age or older, males, members of ethnic groups, part-time students, commuting students, and students speaking English as a second language. Additionally, nontraditional students may have completed a General Educational Development (GED) exam rather than graduating high school or required remedial classes before taking core classes for admission to nursing school.

3. B: Because there is a learning curve with all new positions, the newly hired nurse educator should limit committee work to one committee (or the minimum allowed) for the first year or two. Even though this position does not require participation, committee membership is considered during evaluation, and participation helps the nurse to meet others on the faculty, to become active in academic affairs, and to understand the needs of the organization. Committee membership is a good starting point for networking.

4. C: Although the academic structure may vary somewhat from one institution to another, the nurse educator must have a clear understanding of this structure and should follow standard protocols for requests, and this almost always means that requests be made to the chair of the nursing department first. The chair of the nursing department may then take the request to a dean or vice president as appropriate. The chairperson is generally responsible for contractual agreements, such as an agreement for students to have clinical experience in a rehabilitation center.

5. A: Online classes are most suitable for students who are self-motivated and enjoy studying independently and at their own pace. Although online classes may be more convenient for students who are employed, the classes are not necessarily a good match for the students' learning styles. Many students miss the direct interaction with the instructor and other students even though they may be able to communicate online. Ideally, students should have a choice between taking online or traditional classes.

6. C: Nurse educators are usually evaluated on three elements: teaching ability, scholarship activities, and professional service. Professional service may include volunteer activities within the community, such as volunteering at a free clinic or serving on an advisory board, as well as activities related to local, state, and national organizations, including serving on the board of a national nursing organization. Professional service also includes serving on committees within the organization. Teaching ability may encompass all aspects of teaching, including class performance, curriculum development, and learner outcomes. Scholarship activities may involve giving presentations, writing articles, and conducting research.

7. A: The students are the most important element to consider when designing curriculum for a class. The number of students must be considered because different approaches must be made for a large class (30 or more students) compared to a small class. The ages and experiences of the students are also important considerations because students right out of high school may have different study skills and life experiences than those who have been working, especially those working in healthcare. The academic level of the students must also be considered because approaches to teaching will be different for entering freshman and graduate students.

8. D: LinkedIn is a network designed for professionals and professional communications. Members are able to access information about jobs, current trends, professional news, and information about marketing. Facebook is an open social media site that is used for personal communications as well as for special-interest groups, and it is less focused on business. Instagram is geared towards sharing photographs and videos, while Snapchat is a platform for short and temporarily available videos and images, with both also having private messaging tools.

9. B: Giving each student a separate exam with different questions, unless careful item analysis is carried out, may result in test items with varying difficulty levels, and preparing enough questions so that each student can have a separate exam is very time-consuming, so the best choice is to arrange the same questions in random order for each exam because this can be easily managed with a computer program. Warning students does little to change behavior, and spacing students is always a good idea but may not solve the problem.

10. A: When faced with statistical evidence, students are more likely to admit cheating to the nurse educator than if the nurse asks them or accuses them of cheating. Observational reports of cheating are not always accurate because students may appear to be cheating when they are not, and vice versa. Students have developed more sophisticated ways of cheating than simply looking at each other's papers—electronic messaging, tapping, or pen clicking—so instructors must be vigilant.

11. B: When assigned to teach a new subject, the nurse educator should begin by assessing personal knowledge and expertise in the subject to determine if he will be able to present the material in a manner that is understandable to the students and if he will be able to present a personal perspective about the subject. If the nurse educator has a good knowledge base, then he can focus on teaching strategies, but if he does not, then he must engage in research and study in preparation for teaching.

12. D: Although students who are visual or auditory learners may find films a good learning tool, kinesthetic learners may have difficulty mastering the steps of a procedure by simply watching a film. The most effective teaching strategy is to allow the students to have hands-on experience. Providing written steps or an audiotape reinforces visual and auditory learning but does not address kinesthetic learning. The nurse educator should always try to incorporate a variety of teaching strategies to meet the needs of different types of learners.

13. A: Students in their late twenties to early forties are part of the millennial generation and grew up in a fast-paced world with access to many types of technology and often learn in a different way from older generations, so the first step to improving NCLEX passing rates is to assess teaching strategies to determine if the material is being presented in the best way possible. Lectures should be interspersed with other types of strategies, such as hands-on practice or discussion of case studies. Computer-assisted instruction with interactivity may improve retention.

14. A: An initial strategy for any class is an introduction activity that allows students to relax and get to know each other a little. The nurse educator should give a personal introduction and then involve the class in some type of activity, such as introducing each other in pairs or assigning pairs to introduce each other to the class with one interesting piece of information about the other person. A nonverbal activity, such as having people line up in alphabetical order using nonverbal communication only, may be fun and encourage shy students to participate more actively.

15. C: Although the students obviously did not take a serious approach to the task, their list would make an excellent basis for a serious discussion about nursing stereotypes and preconceived ideas. For example, the class might discuss salaries for nurses compared to physicians and their different roles in the medical community. The class could discuss drug diversion and problems associated with drugs in healthcare. Although nursing is a serious profession, not everything has to be dealt with in a serious manner.

16. A: The theory of behaviorism, developed by Watson, building on the works of Pavlov, includes the use of positive reinforcement, such as praise or rewards, to elicit behavioral changes or desired behavior. However, negative reinforcement can also elicit behavioral changes, so using negative reinforcement should be avoided, and negative outcomes should be ignored, if possible. Although Watson believed that people could be completely controlled by positive reinforcement, other theorists disagree. Concepts of behaviorism are often combined with other theories of learning.

17. D: According to Gagne's nine events associated with instruction, the first event is gaining the attention of the students to activate receptors in the brain. Next, the nurse educator informs the students about objectives and encourages recall of prior learning. The nurse then presents content and provides guidance in the learning procedure, eliciting practice, providing feedback, assessing performance, and enhancing student retention of information by periodic review.

18. B: The theory of deep learning comprises three aspects: deep learning, surface learning, and strategic learning. Surface learning involves memorizing facts, figures, and details to meet some goal, such as passing a test, but the motivation is extrinsic. Deep learning, on the other hand, involves intrinsic motivation and the desire to understand concepts and apply information. Students relate new learning to earlier learning and experiences. Strategic learning is a combination of surface and deep learning because the student does everything needed to master information.

19. B: Keller's ARCS model of motivating students includes the following:

- A—Attention: gained by perceptual (surprise) or inquiry (stimulating curiosity) arousal
- R—Relevance: gained by appealing to students' experience, current value, future value, needs, modeling, and choice
- C—Confidence: gained by allowing students to succeed by providing objectives and prerequisites, to advance, to receive feedback, and to be in control
- S—Satisfaction: gained by providing feedback and opportunities to use knowledge; may be extrinsic or intrinsic and is based on motivation

20. C: Social cognitive theory (Bandura) is based on the idea that the individual learns through reciprocal interactions with the environment, behavior, and cognition and that changing one facet will change the others. The primary method of learning is observation of others. Modeling and outcome expectancies are important components of social cognitive theory, and teachers are expected to serve in the role of models to build a sense of self-efficacy in students through goal setting and self-regulation. Outcomes, according to this theory, are directly influenced by the students' environments.

21. C: According to Van Manen's theory of pedagogy, the basis of teaching is the parent/child relationship. The instructor (in the role of parent) helps to nurture the student and assist the student to grow and develop in an ethical atmosphere. Caring is an important concept of this theory, even though caring and worrying are interrelated. The instructor assumes a responsibility toward the student and the student's welfare and learning. The more the instructor cares, the more the instructor worries about the student.

22. A: Andragogy involves the teaching of adult students who may gain insight from life experiences that younger students lack. Adult students are more self-directed in study and autonomous, depending less on the instructor to provide information. Adult students usually have a clear goal in mind for studying but have many life demands outside of school, such as work and family, and these may interfere with studies. Adult learners often retain information for long periods because they self-initiate learning.

23. A: Although the nurse supervisor may be basing her opinions on stereotyping, bias, and poor judgment, this is primarily an example of discrimination, and it's unlikely she would have the same concerns about male doctors. As males have entered nursing—a profession that for many years was exclusively female—they have faced discrimination and sometimes comments about their motivation and sexual orientation. It is critical that male nurses be treated the same as female nurses and that discrimination be dealt with appropriately.

24. B: According to Quirk's classifications of teaching styles, using experience as a beginning point and then asking students to do further research is an example of suggestive teaching. An assertive approach is usually focused on content and passing of information, such as through lectures. A collaborative approach involves providing the student with problem-solving exercises to promote critical thinking. A facilitative approach challenges the students to develop and use learning skills and to demonstrate skills.

25. A: Kolb's learning style inventory classifies student learning styles based on a learning cycle that includes a cycle of four stages: concrete experience, reflective observation, abstract conceptualization, and active experimentation. Although progressing through all stages is a necessary component of learning, some people prefer a particular style of learning:

- Accommodative: prefer concrete experience with active practice and experimentation
- Divergent: prefer concrete experience and reflective observation
- Assimilative: prefer observation and abstract concepts
- Convergent: prefer abstract concepts and active practice and experimentation

26. D: Horizontal/lateral violence occurs when colleagues or peers use intimidation, verbal abuse, rudeness, or even physical attacks toward one another. People may blame others or bully them into complying with their demands. Horizontal violence may be overt or covert. Horizontal violence serves to erode self-confidence and makes for a hostile work environment, increasing absenteeism and lowering staff morale. Studies show that more than half of nurses have experienced horizontal violence in the workplace. Each institution should have a code of conduct and a plan in place for dealing with horizontal violence.

27. D: A learning objective should include a specific time frame ("By the end of the training session"), the intended student ("the nursing student"), the action ("will demonstrate"), procedure ("correct handwashing techniques"), place ("in all clinical and instructional settings"), and criterion ("100% of the time"). The learning objective is a clear statement of a goal or targeted outcome and is usually included as part of a lesson plan. This type of learning outcome may be better suited to processes than to general knowledge.

28. A: The primary purpose of a lesson plan is to make sure that students meet educational goals. The plan is essentially an outline of the steps that the instructor and students will take to meet these goals and should include the time frame, the expected learner outcomes, the teaching strategy (such as a lecture, presentation of case study, simulation practice), the methods of assessment, as well as any materials used (such as books, slide show presentations, films, simulators, or equipment).

29. B: Although collaborative learning promotes learning and encourages students to work with others, some students are resistive to group work and others fail to contribute adequately to the group effort. The best solution is to give students a group grade that reflects the quality of the project that the students developed as well as an individual grade that reflects the individual's contribution to the project. This may require additional supervision or may require that the students indicate—either in writing or verbally—which parts of the finished project they were responsible for.

30. B: The nurse educator should be a facilitator during group discussions, allowing spontaneous contributions and calling on students at random to answer questions, such as "Thomas, what do you think about Mary's suggestion?" to ensure that all students contribute. In free-form discussions, students may veer from the topic, so some guidance is usually indicated; however, group discussions are effective methods of increasing critical thinking, enhancing learning, and fostering peer support, although they may be a more time-consuming method of transmitting information.

31. C: Ethical issues can arise when students do reflective journals and share private information. In this case, the best initial response is for the nurse to immediately meet with the student who has entrusted him with this information to support her, gain more information about the problem, and explain the organizational procedures that must be followed for substance abuse. The nurse educator should help the student through the process so she can receive appropriate help.

32. D: Role-playing that is designed to provide a simulated interaction between a nursing student and a patient helps the students to understand and empathize with others and gives them a chance to practice interactions and to receive feedback. During role-playing, the students should assume the role of the nurse and the patient, if possible, because this helps the students see the interaction from both perspectives. Following the role-playing exercise, the participants and the observers should debrief, discussing positive and negative observations and exploring how the participants felt during the interaction.

33. C: Working with simulators is surprisingly stressful for some students, especially if changes in simulated conditions happen rapidly, so the nurse should focus on the process and not on the students: "Let's talk about where things went wrong." Debriefing in a nonjudgmental manner can be an excellent teaching tool and gives the students a chance to explore alternate and more effective responses before they try the simulation again. The students are generally aware that they have "killed" the patient and didn't follow nursing procedures, so pointing that out only increases their anxiety.

34. D: Interactivity is the most important consideration when designing modules for computer-assisted instruction because if students only need to read, they can do that just as easily from a book. The advantage to computer-assisted instruction is that the students can be questioned about the material and receive immediate feedback about their mastery of the material. If they answer incorrectly, they can review the same or supplementary material before they proceed. The nurse educator should ensure that the font size is large so that reading is easy and ensure that the layout and color scheme are simple and not distracting.

35. C: Mentoring involves not only guiding students with career activities but also supporting them psychosocially. Career mentoring can include guiding, coaching, networking, modeling, and promoting, whereas psychosocial mentoring can include supporting, inspiring, and empowering. Mentoring educators tend to be participative, encouraging the students to participate actively in their own learning and providing them with as many learning opportunities as possible. The primary goal of mentoring is to allow the student to develop to their full potential.

36. D: Slide shows should have limited explanations (one to five words per topic is preferable) and bulleted lists and should avoid long narratives because students tend to focus on the slides and not the instructor and may miss important information. Font size should be large enough to be easily read from the back of the room, and the nurse educator should try to avoid using different styles and colors of fonts because that may be distracting. The slides should be an outline of the content of a presentation, not the entire content.

37. B: Video podcasting (vodcasting) is an excellent method of recording lectures so students can access them at a later time if they have missed the class or want to review the material. Vodcasting requires a video recording device, built into many computers, and a digital film-editing program, such as iMovie. Once edited, the video is uploaded to a hosting website, such as iTunes, where students can access the video and stream or download it to their own computers or other devices (such as smartphones or tablets).

38. D: Examining the wound for signs of infection is a cause-focused response, which seeks to understand the reason the patient is having increased pain. A solution-focused response is to simply give pain medication or take measures to reduce the patient's discomfort. Nursing students should be taught to consider solution- and cause-focused responses to problem-solving because too often, nurses focus only on solving the problem at hand and may miss complications or opportunities to identify and resolve underlying concerns, such as a patient's fear and anxiety.

39. A: There is clear (level I) evidence that better outcomes are achieved if students are able to demonstrate skills prior to performing them, so this is an element of evidence-based nursing education. Most often, this is accomplished by the use of simulators for such things as giving enemas, inserting catheters, inserting nasogastric tubes, and inserting intravenous lines. Students gain confidence and are less anxious about performing procedures, and patients are subjected to less trial and error.

40. B: Visual learners need to be able to look at something, such as written materials, slide show presentations, demonstrations, films, and visual aids, to help them process information. Auditory learners, however, rely on what they have heard, so they do well with lectures, podcasts, and audiotapes. Kinesthetic learners need to manipulate materials and learn best by doing, so they often do well with simulations. Many people have combined learning styles, such as visual and auditory. Conducting a learning styles inventory can help make the instructor and the students aware of the best way for them to process information.

41. C: International students are often not familiar with multiple-choice tests because written essay exams are more common in many countries. Thus, the most effective strategy is likely to be a workshop on test-taking to help the students develop a strategy for answering multiple-choice questions, especially because the students did well on the essay exam. In fact, all students may benefit from the workshop because many students lack test-taking skills even though they may be familiar with the testing format.

42. C: The nurse educator should conduct a class about proxemics and cultural differences. Americans often assume that personal space is viewed in the same way by all cultures, but there are major differences. The most common American proxemics include:

- Public space: 12–25 feet from the audience
- Social space/business interactions/stranger separation: 4–12 feet
- Personal space/family communications/standing in line: 2–4 feet
- Intimate space/touching/embracing: 0–1 foot

In much of the Middle East, social space is the same as Americans' intimate space. In some countries, such as Germany and the Netherlands, people's personal space extends further.

43. A: Disadvantaged students often lack study skills and may be deficient in social skills as well, making it more difficult for them to succeed. When a school makes a commitment to enroll disadvantaged students, it should also provide them with support that will help them to successfully complete the program. In this case, establishing a study support group in which students can be guided to develop academic skills and can learn how much, how, and when to study may make a profound difference.

44. D: A course syllabus is a legal contract outlining course content and the responsibilities of the instructor and the students. Some schools use a template, whereas others allow more variation, but the nurse educator should follow the usual format. A course syllabus usually includes the course description, course objectives, expected outcomes (measurable), required materials and textbooks, assignments, policies (including absences, grading, and academic integrity), instructor information (office hours, telephone number, and email address), evaluation methods, and detailed course schedule (daily/weekly).

45. B: Once a syllabus is given to the class (usually at the first meeting) and posted, it becomes a legal document, and the grading criteria cannot be changed; therefore, the nurse educator must ensure that the syllabus reads exactly as intended. Although the nurse educator must use the grading criteria established on the syllabus, the nurse may change the criteria at the end of the academic session for the next incoming class. Additionally, the nurse educator must adhere to all policies established in the syllabus and apply them equally to all students.

46. A: Behavioral objectives include psychomotor, cognitive, and affective objectives:

- Psychomotor: Tasks and specific skills, such as inserting a Foley catheter, irrigating a colostomy, and changing a wound dressing. Verbs include demonstrate, show, use, and administer.
- Cognitive: Empirical knowledge and information, such as the characteristic of a disease, side effects of drugs, and usual treatment for a condition. Verbs include arrange, classify, categorize, identify, diagram, explain, compare, and diagnose.
- Affective: Values, feelings, and beliefs. Verbs include appreciate, value, and recognize.

47. B: Bloom's original taxonomy (1956) includes six domains of cognitive learning:

- Knowledge: requires recall of facts and information (list, select, choose, and define)
- Comprehension: requires the ability to make interpretations and comparisons and to understand information (explain, compare, and outline)
- Application: requires the ability to solve problems and use new information (identify, use, and apply)

- Analysis: requires the ability to make inferences from information and the ability to find evidence (examine, find, analyze, and evaluate)
- Synthesis: requires the ability to draw information from multiple sources and find solutions to problems (predict, formulate, and create)
- Evaluation: requires the ability to make judgments and propose valid ideas (interpret, evaluate, and conclude)

48. C: For new nurse educators, the greatest challenge is often time allocation because, until the nurse has taught a course or done lessons, it can be very difficult to determine how much time to allocate for an activity. Things may go wrong, equipment sometimes doesn't work, discussions often don't go as planned, and disruptions can occur. When designing a course and developing lessons, the nurse educator should allocate extra time for class activities. In some cases, such as lectures, the nurse may time a practice session, but this is often not practical and is too time-consuming to do for every class.

49. C: The average adult attention span is about 15–20 minutes. This means that if the nurse educator has planned a one-hour lecture, then she needs to do something different every 20 minutes or so to retain the students' attention. The lecture doesn't have to stop completely, but the pace should be varied. The nurse might take a minute to review the main points already covered with a slide show presentation, allow for a question/answer period, show a short film, take a "stretch" break, or encourage discussion.

50. D: The nurse educator often has to cover material with which she may not be familiar. The nurse educator should always research the material and ask for the advice of others, but in this case, the best solution is to arrange for a hospice nurse to be a guest speaker because hospice care is an emotional topic and students often feel anxious about caring for dying patients and can benefit from the real-life experiences of a hospice nurse. The nurse educator must first review administrative policies about guest speakers.

51. A: The free clinic is probably the best placement for nursing students to observe and gain knowledge of community health needs because it likely serves a population with a variety of health concerns, whereas the other organizations serve limited populations or see patients only briefly. Some free clinics, such as RotaCare, are sponsored by organizations and staffed by volunteers, whereas others have paid staff. The type of care provided may vary widely from one type of clinic to another, so the nurse educator must assess each one to determine if it meets the needs of the students.

52. C: Although reading assignments vary widely, generally, upper division students (junior, senior level) are expected to be able to read 100 to 150 pages per week for a class, and reading assignments should not exceed these numbers, especially considering that students may have multiple classes. However, the nurse should evaluate the content of books when assigning readings because the number of words per page may also vary widely depending on font size, illustrations, and other features of texts.

53. B: Although there are many advantages to this type of system, the primary advantage for the instructor and students is ease of access. Most students now have laptops, and they can access course materials at any time and can upload assignments from home rather than taking them to class. The system may save time in some instances, such as with record-keeping, but preparing good materials for the course management system may require an extra investment in time for the instructor.

54. D: Exams that are recorded electronically, whether on a computer or through the use of a Scantron machine, are the easiest to analyze because the calculations do not need to be done manually. Many exam programs are able to generate not only individual student scores but also class average scores, reliability scores, and item analysis. This type of grading and analysis is appropriate for answers that are quantifiable. Essay questions, on the other hand, must be evaluated separately.

55. D: By far, the best preparation for developing an online course is to take an online course and experience firsthand what works well and what doesn't. Developing an online course can be quite complex because content must be developed; multimedia incorporated; and interactivity, evaluation, and assessment planned carefully to create an effective course. The nurse educator should also research online formats and discuss online offerings with experienced instructors. Many online course delivery systems have templates that must be used during course design.

56. A: The most effective teaching strategy for abstract concepts is to use real-life, concrete examples to help students find meaning. For example, if discussing the abstract concept of a caring environment, the nurse educator may use an example of a nurse who contacted an animal shelter to find a temporary home with "foster parents" for the pet of an elderly patient who was hospitalized. Students can often relate to concrete examples better than abstract philosophical discussions.

57. D: Although all of these are important, the most critical is the course content. Students can readily ascertain if the instructor is not prepared and does not have adequate background information about the course she is teaching, resulting in a loss of confidence in the instructor. Therefore, the nurse educator must learn the content as well as possible before teaching by whatever means necessary—reading, researching, shadowing, consulting—and gather materials to support the students' learning. The nurse educator may not be an expert in the content, but she should be proficient.

58. B: The initial action for a committee asked to redesign courses is to conduct a thorough review of the literature about problem-based learning to gain as much background knowledge as possible. The members should contact others using problem-based learning for input and should gather information from other sources, such as at national conferences. Implementation is best done in stages, such as in one or a small number of classes initially, so the results can be analyzed.

59. B: A critical element of objective structured clinical evaluation (OSCE) is that, as much as possible, all students should have the same experience at each station and be asked the same questions. With OSCE, several stations are set up. Students move from one station to the next with a limited time (usually 5 to 10 minutes) at each station. If electronic simulators are used, they should have the same settings for each student. If people serve as simulated patients, they should follow the same script, using the same words and expressing the same emotions for each student.

60. C: The best solution is to establish a tutoring program to assist students in the course. Anatomy and physiology courses require a lot of memorization and are difficult for many students, resulting in its often acting as a "gatekeeper" course, serving to eliminate unqualified students. Lowering standards by accepting a lower grade or allowing more repetitions of a required course is rarely a good solution because admitting unqualified students sets them up for failure of nursing classes or the NCLEX. Taking no action may result in the loss of potential candidates for the school of nursing.

61. A: Formative evaluations are usually conducted while a course is in progress to determine the effectiveness of teaching and whether students are learning and understanding concepts and procedures. The nurse educator may use the results to assess whether students need further instruction or clinical experience. Depending on the results, she may revise teaching strategies or provide supplementary materials to help the students meet expected outcomes. Summative evaluations are given at the end of a course and are generally used to determine grades.

62. D: In developing psychomotor skills, the first step is imitation, during which the student learns by watching and copying what another is demonstrating. Step two, manipulation, comprises guided practice to improve skills. Step three, precision, occurs when the student can perform a task without referring to a guide or asking for assistance. Step four, articulation, occurs when the student is able to combine more than one skill. The last step, naturalization, represents the ability to do steps in sequence automatically because the skills have become innate.

63. A: The one-minute paper is an assignment that is routinely used in many classes to assess the effectiveness of the class. The students are usually asked to answer two questions in one minute:

- What is the most important thing you learned in this class?
- What is still unclear to you?

The nurse educator then uses these responses to modify teaching strategies or determine which topics need further elaboration or practice. The nurse educator may receive positive and negative feedback about his or her teaching.

64. C: The three R's of mentoring are reflecting, reframing, and resolving:

- Reflecting: Discussing previous and/or shared experiences, setting ground rules, getting to know each other, sharing information, and establishing goals. The mentor must practice active listening and ask questions of the student.
- Reframing: Evaluating and providing feedback so the student can gain competence. The mentor encourages the student to come up with solutions to problems.
- Resolving: Developing new problem-solving skills and action plans that allow the student to act independently.

65. A: Although there is value to all of these strategies, the best strategy is to provide clear directions and writing samples for all writing assignments. Virtually all nursing programs require students to take college-level writing courses, and many require competency tests, but students often lack writing skills. However, skills can improve with practice, especially if students have a clear understanding of what is expected of them in terms of format, word length, and point of view.

66. B: Ecological validity (a form of external validity) considers the effect that the environment of testing has on students' behavior. Validity may be high if students are taking a type of test with which they are familiar in an environment that they are used to. However, validity may be affected if the testing changes from, for example, a paper test to a computerized test or from a classroom to an auditorium. Students' anxiety or nervousness about a change may affect their performance.

67. D: Evaluating validity based on personal opinion is an example of face validity. Face validity is the weakest form of validity because it is based on subjective analysis, but it is also one of the most commonly used. Face validity suggests that a test looks valid and appears to test what it is supposed to test. Content validity is based on the evaluation of experts, who generally use statistical analysis to determine if a test actually covers the content adequately.

68. A: The nurse educator should begin hierarchical task analysis by creating a list of all of the tasks involved in a process (usually up to five) and then grouping the tasks according to similarities. A single task may be represented in more than one group. Once the grouping is done, the nurse educator should evaluate and regroup as needed, referring to experts as necessary throughout the process. Once the groups are in place, the nurse educator then further evaluates and organizes the tasks in a hierarchical manner in each group.

69. C: Krathwhol's affective taxonomy is as follows:

- Receiving: accepting, listening to, differentiating, or responding to a situation or event
- Responding: complying with, following, commending, or in some way responding to the situation or event
- Valuing: relinquishing, supporting, debating, or valuing the event or situation
- Organization: discussing, theorizing, or examining the values in terms of those values already held to internalize them
- Characterization by value or value complex: revising, requiring, avoiding, resisting, or resolving to act according to internalized values

70. B: A simulation exercise is an example of authentic assessment that involves the performance of authentic tasks that mimic, as much as possible, real-life experiences. Authentic assessment involves five dimensions: the assessment task as designed by the nurse educator, the physical context (such as a hospital room), the social context, the assessment results, and the assessment criteria (which should be similar to those used in actual clinical situations). Students should have a clear understanding of assessment criteria prior to beginning the task.

71. B: Even if a clinical evaluation tool has content validity, that does not ensure interinstructor reliability. Multiple instructors (two or more) should use the clinical evaluation tool to evaluate the same group of students (ideally 30 or more) and then to compare results. Where differences occur in the student ratings, the instructors should discuss the results to determine if the instructors understand the grading criteria and if the tool should be modified to ensure greater consistency.

72. A: The initial concern when planning the clinical rotation for a student in a wheelchair is to determine which accommodations are necessary to allow the student to participate fully. Although staff support is important, acceptance often comes with experience. Whereas some modifications in the caseload may be necessary, generally students with disabilities are expected to carry similar caseloads. In some cases, students with disabilities may need assistance with some tasks, such as reaching things placed on high shelves, although another student is not usually assigned specifically to assist.

73. B: Instituting a pilot program is often an excellent way to ensure that faculty members support changes because many people are resistive to changes. A pilot program initiated on a small scale can provide feedback that can be used to modify or revise the program as needed before instituting the program for the entire department because new curriculum design is rarely without problems. Those involved in the pilot program can also then serve as mentors to others.

74. D: Leadership is an essential skill for those involved in curriculum development because they must work with other faculty and also help initiate changes that faculty may be resistant to. Education may focus initially on what comprises leadership, various leadership styles (including pros and cons), and leadership responsibilities in the development of curriculum, including planning and conducting meetings, researching, and networking with others. Those with leadership experience and abilities may be used as mentors to assist in developing other leaders.

75. C: Before initiating curriculum development activities on a large scale, the committee should select a change theory to serve as a guide or framework. Change theories generally propose several steps to follow to bring about change. Following a change theory can keep the process from becoming too scattered. For example, Kotter's eight-stage process begins with creating a sense of urgency and taking control of the process and then building a group of stakeholders to build trust and work toward a common goal before taking direct actions toward curriculum development.

76. D: The best solution to encourage staff support and participation in curriculum design is to establish several ad hoc committees comprised of staff members because when people participate in a project, they become active stakeholders and are more likely to be supportive of the end product. The ad hoc committees are short-term, so they do not require long-term investments in time and are usually assigned discrete tasks, such as gathering data or writing outcomes for a course.

77. B: Quantifying organizational culture is difficult, so the best data collection method is to review documents such as vision and mission statements and organizational charts because this can provide information about processes for decision-making and internal and external relationships. Interviews with key personnel, such as administrators, committee chairpersons, and program directors can also provide valuable information about values and how people in the organization interact as well as how open staff members are to change.

78. C: Finding adequate financial resources is often a problem when upgrading to new and expensive equipment. The initial strategy should be to research grants because money may be available from other sources. Even if the nurse educator is only able to gain a grant for part of the needed money, the administration may be more willing to reconsider if the organization does not need to bear the entire cost. The nurse educator may also research other sources of financial support, such as community agencies or corporations.

79. A: Pre- and posttests that focus on critical thinking skills may provide the best information because the results are quantifiable and help to evaluate changes in a group of students over a period of time. Student and nursing staff surveys are more subjective and may not provide an accurate picture of the students' skill levels. Students may not be able to do effective self-evaluation, and nursing staff may be biased. Observations are limited in effectiveness because they are usually done for short periods.

80. C: Because both male and female nursing students are dropping out of the program during the obstetrics-gynecology (OB-GYN) clinical rotation, this is not a gender issue. The initial action should be to design and conduct a learner needs evaluation to determine what changes in the program can be instituted to reduce the dropout rate. As part of the evaluation, interviews or surveys may be conducted with students who have dropped out to determine their reasons.

81. B: The primary advantage to using an internal evaluator for program assessment is that the internal evaluator has a better overall understanding of the program and may be aware of issues that an external evaluator may overlook. An internal evaluator may also be better able to provide feedback; however, the internal evaluator may also be biased, relying on subjective opinion, which can reduce the credibility of the assessment. Typically, external evaluators are believed to provide more objective evaluations.

82. D: The curriculum redesign committee needs input from a variety of sources including faculty, employers, community agencies, current students, and graduates, so the best strategy is likely to begin with focus groups to explore what the students need and what is missing. For example, employers may focus on the skills that new hires lack and the length of time and expense involved in training new staff, whereas students and graduates may focus on areas in which they feel insecure regarding their knowledge.

83. D: The accreditation model focuses on standards established by accrediting agencies to determine if the program corresponds to the vision and mission statement and if it meets the goals and expected outcomes. Evidence-based evaluation and self-evaluation are integral components that are used to identify opportunities for improvement and to promote continuous quality improvement of the program. Accrediting agencies for schools of nursing include the Accreditation Commission for Education in Nursing and the Commission on Collegiate Nursing Education.

84. B: National standardized tests (such as the National Council Licensure Examination [NCLEX]) usually have a reliability coefficient of 0.9 and above on a scale that ranges from 1.0 (completely reliable) to 0 (completely unreliable). A very good classroom examination should score between 0.8 to 0.9 and generally does not require revision. A score of 0.7 to 0.8 (the most common range for classroom examinations) means that the test has good reliability but a few questions may be too hard or too easy and should be revised. A score of 0.5 to 0.6 generally means that the examination should be revised unless it is very short (<10 questions).

85. A: Examination questions can be categorized as follows:

- Application: focuses on students providing characteristics, guidelines, rules, lists, and principles as well as carrying out procedures and calculations according to sets of rules or steps
- Analysis: focuses on differentiating, identifying, distinguishing, and discriminating based on information to reach decisions
- Synthesis: focuses on designing, producing, writing, and devising an original product (paper, plan, or project) based on research and knowledge
- Evaluation: focuses on evaluating, judging, comparing, and justifying based on research, information, and observation

86. C: Although students should have equal testing, it is reasonable to allow extended time for test taking for a student with dyslexia who reads and processes words more slowly than others. If the student is easily distracted, the test may be given in a separate room. Additionally, the student may benefit from a review of test-taking strategies because multiple-choice questions, which are commonly used for student assessment, may be difficult for those with dyslexia, and learning these strategies may help the student take tests such as the NCLEX exam.

87. C: Nursing programs should be as inclusive as possible, and this may mean making accommodations for religious beliefs when those accommodations do not endanger patients or staff. The best solution is to meet with the infection control office to develop policies for observant Muslim students who must maintain modesty. It is important to remember that Muslims vary in observance, the same as do those in other religions, and not all will wear the hijab or follow strict rules about modesty.

88. D: Experience alone does not ensure that a person has leadership qualities. The nurse educator's initial action should be to honestly assess his own leadership style and effectiveness by considering how he works with others, how he solves problems, and how he gets along with other people. The nurse educator should also consider his goals in working with a committee and his expectations of others in the group. Once the assessment is completed, he can better determine how to prepare for the leadership role.

89. D: People who are negative and angry often make rude comments in an attempt to goad others into expressing anger, so the best response is "We'd like to hear your ideas. What do you suggest?" This response is not argumentative, and it focuses on what is actually expected of members of the group—participation. If the person is angry because she feels her input isn't valued or that she is ignored, this gives her a chance to talk about her ideas. If the negative comments are a cover for not having anything to contribute, then this response removes that cover.

90. A: The nurse educator should not put career goals on hold but must be realistic about the amount of time required to become comfortable and adept in a new position. The nurse educator should aim to accomplish one or two career goal activities during the first year. These may be in the areas of teaching (such as learning new teaching strategies), scholarship (such as focused studying), and professional activities (such as attending a national conference).

91. C: Although there is value in meeting staff, joining organizations, and asking advice, the first step to networking is to inventory personal and professional connections. These can include friends, family, alumni, faculty members, peers, supervisors, administrators, physicians, and other health personnel as well as connections in other fields such as business. The nurse educator should create lists and rank those on the list according to how close the association is and what benefit the nurse can obtain from or provide to the relationship.

92. D: The choice of which job to take depends on many factors, but an important consideration is career goals. It is usually easier to move down than up, so if the eventual goal is to work as a nurse educator in a graduate program, then the baccalaureate program may be the best choice. If the nurse educator's goal is to stay in one position for an extended period or work close to home, then the associate degree program may be the best choice. The nurse educator should get as much information about the schools as possible.

93. B: A breach of duty occurs if a nurse fails to provide a patient with care consistent with basic standards of care for the patient's condition. Duty to client refers to care that the patient is entitled to according to the nurse's employment and standards of care. Causation is the relationship between harm that occurs to the patient and the nurse's failure to meet standards of care. Damage is the direct proof of harm resulting from a nurse's unsafe nursing practice.

94. B: Institutions are held responsible for acts of negligence on the part of employees through vicarious liability because employers are often considered supervisors, and thus they are responsible for ensuring that standards of care are met. However, if an institution must pay damages, the principle of indemnification allows the institution to in turn sue the negligent employee to regain money paid out as damages. Therefore, all supervisory staff members have important roles in helping an institution avoid liability.

95. D: Nonmaleficence is the ethical principle that means that the nurse should not harm the patient; however, in some cases, this principle may be violated for the greater good. In the case of cardiopulmonary resuscitation (CPR), the patient was harmed because of the fractured ribs but survived, so CPR was ultimately for the good of the patient. Nonmaleficence may be violated by many medical procedures, such as amputations and administration of chemotherapy, so the harm to the patient should always be considered in planning care.

96. C: SMART guidelines (Drucker) are often used when setting project, management, and personal goals and objectives:

- S—Specific: Goals should be narrowly outlined, concrete, and clear rather than broad.
- M—Measurable: Outcomes should be stated in measurable/quantifiable terms.
- A—Attainable: Goals should be realistic and possible to attain.
- R—Relevant: Goals should be directed toward results.
- T—Time-oriented: A specific time frame for achieving goals should be defined.

97. A: Discriminating in relation to questions refers to the degree of difficulty. Questions should be difficult enough that some but not all students are able to answer them correctly. Generally, if questions are discriminating, the upper third of students will answer the questions correctly, the middle third will vary with some answering correctly and others not, and the lower third of students will not answer correctly. When evaluating for discrimination, it's important to have an adequate number of students (30 plus is preferable).

98. D: A mentor is invaluable to increase the nurse's socialization to the role of nurse educator because this person is able to help the nurse educator to navigate a new situation and more fully comprehend the orientation. Some programs automatically provide mentors for nurse educators new to a position, but the nurse educator may, in some cases, need to seek a mentor. An extensive orientation should introduce all faculty and personnel, review courses and administrative structure, and provide the nurse a good understanding of the culture of the organization.

99. B: Although all of these are important, the most important is committing to and engaging in lifelong learning because the field of nursing is dynamic, so knowledge must be continuously updated. Nurse educators must take continuing education courses and increase knowledge in their area of expertise through practice and study. Nurse educators must meet certification requirements but should also pursue advanced degrees when possible. Lifelong learning requires self-directed studies and recognition of the need for ongoing education.

100. A: The primary function of a nurse leader is to serve as a role model for others. This means that the nurse leader must show respect for others, collaborate with other staff members, demonstrate knowledge, follow the nursing code of ethics, and provide excellent nursing care. A nurse educator who wants to be a leader must have personal integrity, a clear vision of the future, and the ability to adequately manage change and inspire others.

101. C: According to Lewin's force field analysis, the first task when planning a change is to consider the driving forces (leadership, incentives, and needs) and the restraining forces (finances, negativity, and lack of equipment). The nurse educator lists the proposed change and then creates two columns, with one labeled "driving forces" and the other labeled "restraining forces." Then, brainstorming is done to identify those forces, followed by discussion and development of a plan to diminish the restraining forces.

102. A: The primary method of showing cultural competence is to demonstrate respect for those with other values and cultures. This usually requires the nurse to seek out opportunities to learn about other cultures and to understand different value systems. Cultural competence also requires that the nurse educator be aware of the attitudes of others and take action to combat prejudice and educate others to be more accepting and tolerant. The nurse educator must ensure that issues related to cultural competence are incorporated into teaching.

103. C: Scholarship is a process of inquiry or study that leads to specific outcomes. A prime example of recognition of scholarship is receiving a grant or other type of award, such as for excellence in teaching. Other forms of recognition include having scholarly works published in journals or books or being asked to serve as a consultant, presenter, or mentor to share expertise. Recognition may be tied to financial gain, such as when merit raises are given, but rewards are often less tangible.

104. B: Advocacy is an important role for the nurse educator, who must advocate for the profession, the students, and the patients. As an advocate for the profession, the nurse must take an active role in organizations such as the American Nurses Association as well as in the political arena, helping to formulate and support legislation that positively impacts nursing. As an advocate for students, the nurse educator must ensure that students receive the best possible education, and as an advocate for patients, the nurse educator must serve as a role model to ensure excellence in care.

105. D: The primary purpose of the American Nurses Advocacy Institute is to train nurses to become political leaders. The American Nurses Association (ANA) sponsors this program, which is a 12-month mentored program. To be eligible for the program, the nurse must be a member of the ANA and the state nursing association. The nurse is trained to serve as an advisor to state nursing associations regarding political strategies and as an educator of others in the profession.

106. A: The Affordable Care Act has a strong focus on prevention and the promotion of wellness. Patients need to know what preventive services are available to them, and nurses need to be better educated about preventive medicine. Many preventive services that were not covered by insurance policies or required a copayment or deductible are now available without cost. Screenings include abdominal aortic aneurysm screening for men who have smoked, alcohol screening, colorectal cancer screening for adults over age 50, diabetes (type 2) screening for adults with a history of hypertension, human immunodeficiency virus (HIV) screening, and immunizations.

107. C: The process model of assessment focuses on the way things are done rather than the outcomes. This model often looks closely at efficiency and the quantity and quality of the work process and tries to identify the need for changes in processes to make the organization more financially stable. One problem with the focus on processes is that outcomes may be overlooked and care compromised when too much focus is placed on cost saving.

108. D: The five stages of acceptance are (1) knowledge, (2) persuasion, (3) decision, (4) implementation, and (5) confirmation. The first stage—knowledge—is critical because it lays the foundation upon which the nurse is able to persuade others. The nurse educator should begin by doing research and providing facts and figures, case studies, and research findings to support the innovation. People should be given time to study the information and ask questions so they do not feel like they are being rushed or forced.

109. B: The most critical element of peer evaluation is for the evaluator to provide concrete examples to support scoring so students can understand their strengths and weaknesses. Feedback is usually provided after an evaluation, not during the evaluation. Although fully completing the form and doing it in a timely manner are also important, it is more important that the evaluation serve as a learning tool and help the student improve skills.

110. C: CINAHL is a database that contains full-text journals in the nursing and allied health fields, with records dating from 1937 to the present. CINAHL requires a subscription, but many academic libraries have subscriptions that allow students and faculty access. Different versions of CINAHL are available. The basic CINAHL subscription contains access to 70 full-text journals from 1993 to the present, and the more expensive CINAHL Complete contains 1325 full-text journals from 1937 to the present, as well as evidence-based care sheets, a drug guide, patient handouts, and lessons.

111. B: The most important factor to ensuring adequate assessment is to use the same outcomes assessment tool and scoring criteria. Faculty are rarely required to have exactly the same course content or to use the same teaching methods in class because this interferes with their autonomy as instructors, but they need to be cognizant of the need to adequately prepare students to meet the learning outcomes. Grading standards may vary from one instructor to another, but this is a separate issue from assessing learning outcomes.

112. A: The best use of student learning outcomes data is to assess the overall effectiveness of the curricula. Outcomes data should not be used in a punitive manner to rank faculty or as part of the evaluation process. In some cases, individual faculty may receive results, but in many cases, specific information about individual students and faculty is not provided, depending on the school policy. However, all faculty should receive the overall results and use this information to identify areas of strengths and weaknesses.

113. A: Studies have shown that the ability to respect different viewpoints and to discuss diverse perspectives are critical leadership skills. Working on group projects regarding sociocultural issues gives students the opportunity to practice listening and speaking as well as collaboration because an effective group presentation and discussion requires that all members cooperate and contribute. Nurse educators should provide students many opportunities to develop leadership skills, and this may include assessing the students' leadership styles.

114. C: The best first step is for the experienced educator to observe the nurse educator teaching a class, carefully observing class interactions, student responses, pacing of lessons, and teaching strategies. These observations can then serve as the basis for a discussion about what was more successful and what was less successful, beginning with how the less experienced nurse educator felt about the class. The experienced nurse should keep his comments positive (focusing on strengths rather than weaknesses) and constructive and should avoid criticism.

115. C: External validity refers to the degree to which research findings are generalizable. Research findings should be replicable in different settings and with different groups of patients. Most research projects aim for external validity. For example, if a nursing procedure is found to be effective for one group of patients, other nurses may want to apply the findings to their patients; therefore, it is especially important that the sample characteristics of the subject, the environment, and the research situation are adequate.

116. B: The most effective method of controlling intrinsic factors related to research subjects is randomization. Randomization is essential to obtaining comparable groups in terms of extraneous variables, which may vary depending on the research project. Subjects must be assigned to a control or experimental group by random. This can be achieved in various ways (e.g., drawing names or flipping coins), but the most common method is to use a computer program to randomize subjects or to use a table of random numbers.

117. A: The nurse educator should act proactively by identifying cost-cutting measures before they are mandated by the administration. Although justifying budgetary expenses is also important, all departments will be doing the same, and this does little to solve the problem of inadequate financial resources. Nursing programs are vulnerable because the student-to-instructor ratio is often smaller than for other types of programs. Nurse educators may need to be creative, such as by creating community partnerships, to maintain the nursing program.

118. D: The primary focus when instituting change should be on finding and using the best available evidence-based research. However, the nurse educator should also consider the expertise of those involved, such as faculty members; the resources (financial, social, and psychological) that are available; the characteristics of those involved; the environment; the organizational structure; the mission and values of the institution; and the impact any changes will have on those affected by the changes, such as staff, administration, and students.

119. B: An observational learning experience is a type of clinical experience that provides education but does not involve direct contact or interaction with patients. Observing an autopsy or a surgical procedure is an example. During an observational learning experience, the student watches and listens. The student may take notes as well. The observational learning experience is usually tied to an assignment, such as a written or oral report about what the student has observed and learned.

120. D: If a student is in class eight hours per week, then he should have 24 clinical hours with an established ratio of 1:3. Schools may have slightly different ratios, but the nurse must keep the required ratios in mind when planning courses and clinical experiences for students. The hours may be calculated according to total semester or quarter hours. In some cases, students may spend more hours in class initially and then increase clinical hours, but they should always maintain the total hours within the ratio over the duration of the semester or quarter.

121. C: The recommendation of the Institute of Medicine (IOM) is that 80% of the total nursing workforce obtain at least a baccalaureate degree in nursing by the year 2020. While acknowledging the contributions of vocational/practical nurses and nurses with associate degrees, the IOM feels that a more highly educated nursing workforce is necessary to provide excellence in patient care and improved access to care. As part of lifelong learning, nurses are encouraged to continue working toward a baccalaureate degree after graduation from a vocational/practical or associate degree nursing program.

122. B: Assisting with triage at a school is likely to best help nursing students address the Quality and Safety Education for Nurses (QSEN) competency of interdisciplinary collaboration and teamwork because the nursing students will have to cooperate with many different disciplines. The police will be there to assist, block off the area, and manage the crowds, especially parents coming to the school in search of their children. The fire department will be carrying out rescues and bringing patients to the triage area. Paramedics will be transporting patients. Psychologists and social workers may be present to provide assistance to faculty, family members, and traumatized children.

123. B: The most appropriate action is to fail the student, keeping in mind that students have a right to fail. The nurse educator has made efforts to assist the student, but the student has persisted in turning in papers late, showing a lack of responsibility. There may be valid reasons why the student has been unable to keep up in class, but giving the student special consideration is unfair to the other students who did turn in their work on time.

124. D: Wearing gloves when assisting a patient to use a bedpan supports the Joint Commission's goal of reducing the risk of healthcare-associated infection. Alcohol-based skin cleansers may be used to cleanse the hands but not if the hands are soiled. In that case, the hands must be washed with soap and running water. Dirty linen should never be placed on a floor, and urinals should not be placed on an overbed table with a meal tray.

125. A: Students learn better by actively engaging in an assignment, so asking the students to observe and identify a safety issue in clinical practice and then research evidence-based practices regarding the issue is the best assignment. This increases students' awareness of safety issues—such as failing to use proper hand hygiene or failing to use two identifiers when administering treatment to a patient—and gives them practical experience in researching evidence-based practices.

126. C: The Ishikawa "fishbone" diagram is an analysis tool that is used to analyze cause and effect. It may be used as part of process or performance improvement strategies to identify root causes. The diagram itself has the shape of a fish, with the head being labeled with the effect (or problem) and the bones of the fish labeled with the causes. The causes are categorized according to whether they are related to manufacturing/production, administration, or service.

127. B: The nurse educator cannot have two standards for the same group of students, so assignments must be the same, but the nurse educator should encourage those with healthcare backgrounds to share experiences during discussions because this takes advantage of their experience and allows the other students to learn from them. Rarely do all students have the same level of experience, but experience alone or lack of experience does not always predict the students who need added support.

128. D: Extrinsic motivators are usually those that can be observed or measured, such as a certificate of achievement, a grade, a promotion, a salary increase, improved working situations, or other type of award or reward. Adult learners tend to respond to external and internal motivators, so the nurse educator should consider motivators when planning coursework and assignments. Providing extrinsic motivators may help students develop internal motivators. Internal motivators relate to feelings, such as enjoyment, job satisfaction, and self-esteem.

129. A: "Uses a variety of different feedback and outcomes data to evaluate the effectiveness of the program" is the most appropriate competency statement. The competency statement is an umbrella statement that outlines in general terms what is expected. The competency statement should be based on those elements that will be included in the program evaluation, including such things as measures of staff competency, outcomes data, and staff satisfaction, as well as the expected processes and actions.

130. C: The first thing the committee should do when planning a staff education program is to conduct a needs assessment to determine what type of education program the staff needs and wants. Some topics, such as sexual harassment and cardiopulmonary resuscitation (CPR), may be mandatory, so time must be allowed for these topics. Needs assessments are often done by survey and/or interviews but may also include a review of data to determine areas of weakness. Once topics are identified, then goals and objectives as well as assessment methods are determined. Cost-effectiveness is a consideration when planning how to present the topics.

131. D: Operational integration has been achieved when staff members exhibit changes in behavior resulting from the education program. This is a more effective measure than learning demonstrated through assessment because staff members may know the material and be able to provide a demonstration within a class framework but still not integrate it into work situations. Staff satisfaction is not always a good measure of effectiveness because staff may consider such elements as time and compensation. Meeting goals and objectives is important when considering cost effectiveness.

132. A: Although ancillary study materials are helpful, they often review the book content or provide practice, so assigning the ancillary material may not promote use. The best approach is for the nurse educator to conduct a class orientation to show students how to access and use the material, stressing ways in which the material may help them to learn and improve their grades (extrinsic motivation). Studies show that ancillary electronic materials are rarely used effectively, if at all.

133. C: Student-centered learning is an active form of learning that requires the student to be engaged in the learning process, usually resulting in better retention of information and more effective learning. However, many students actually prefer the passive learning approach in which the instructor lectures because this requires less effort. Although the instructor's role in class may be minimized, in fact, planning effective student-centered learning activities may be time-consuming and more difficult than planning lectures.

134. D: In unstructured learning or inquiry-based learning, the student learns through experience and observation with no or minimal direction from the nurse educator. For example, when attending an Alcoholics Anonymous (AA) meeting, the student is able to learn about the processes used in AA, the types of interactions that occur, the types of people who are participating, and the purposes. The student may have the opportunity to meet the participants and socialize, using communication skills and gaining understanding.

135. A: The most effective learning activity to develop the affective domain is for the student to present a case study related to teaching a patient and his family about disease prevention. The affective domain is related to people's feelings and attitudes, so teaching disease prevention requires that the student engage the patient and his family in discussions about attitudes toward health and life changes necessary to prevent disease. This process also helps the student to develop an understanding of the attitudes, values, and feelings of the self as well as others.

136. B: Informatics is a growing field within the nursing profession and refers to the handling of information rather than the use of computers or preparation of electronic presentations. All nursing students should have some knowledge of informatics. At the most basic level, instruction should prepare students to access databases and research patient care issues. As students become more adept, they should be able to do more detailed research and use that information to develop evidence-based practices.

137. C: Studies show the transition from clinical nursing to educating can be difficult. Nurse educators go through a stage of anticipation before teaching begins, expecting to be able to make a positive impact on students. The next stage, disorientation, begins when the nurse educator actually starts teaching and realizes that orientation and mentoring are not adequate preparations. The nurse educator may lack the knowledge and skills needed to teach. This is followed by information-seeking, during which the nurse tries to better prepare for teaching. The last stage is formation of identity as a nurse educator.

138. D: The greatest concern related to the shortage of nursing faculty is the age of current nurse educators. Many are nearing retirement age (the average age is older than 51 years), and the number of nurse educators preparing to enter the field is diminishing, partially because salaries are often higher for clinical positions than for academic. Additionally, time constraints may make it difficult for nurse educators to maintain clinical skills, and the numbers of nurses with master's degrees or doctorates has not kept pace with need.

139. B: The nurse educator should be sure to keep careful records, documenting all observations and findings. The evaluations should be as objective as possible and based on direct observations by the nurse educator. The nurse educator should make multiple observations rather than evaluating the student on one observation alone and should be clear about expectations. The nurse educator should allow adequate time for students to achieve goals and should assess for safety and skills.

140. C: Although all of these are concerns, the primary reason for not accepting students into nursing programs is a continued lack of faculty. Many nursing programs are unable to find and hire faculty to fill current positions or proposed positions, preventing expansion of programs, so many students who are academically prepared to enter nursing schools are unable to gain admission. Therefore, the nurse educator must promote the profession among other nurses, encouraging those with good clinical skills and educational background to consider a teaching career.

141. D: Action research is built about a series of cycles that begin with planning and acting to bring about changes. These actions are followed by making observations and the final and most critical action of reflecting on how successful the change has been. A new cycle of planning then begins, using the information gained by the previous cycle and the reflection. Action research can be used on an ongoing basis to facilitate quality improvement in processes.

142. C: The student-created video presentation is most likely to ensure that the information received into short-term memory is encoded into long-term memory because the creation of the video requires active participation and use of the knowledge rather than passive reception. The students may choose various methods of presentation—acting, drawing cartoons, or recording a lecture—but all approaches require that the students study and organize ideas. The nurse educator must use every opportunity to encourage learning rather than focusing on teaching.

143. D: Implicit memory allows students to carry out actions automatically without thought. This is sometimes referred to as "rote" knowledge, and it is a form of long-term memory. Explicit memory and autobiographical memory are also forms of long-term memory. Explicit memory requires that people think about something to elicit a memory, such as when a student actively tries to recall the steps to a procedure. Autobiographical memory relates to those things in one's life that one remembers, such as events and people.

144. A: Philosophies of evaluation orientation include the following:

- Service: Evaluation focuses on the strengths and weaknesses of the student to help him or her progress.
- Practice: This model focuses primarily on end results: the ability of students at the end of a course to meet outcomes objectives.
- Judgmental: Evaluation focuses on grading, pass or fail, and the results of testing.
- Constructivist: This model allows input from a variety of sources that have a vested interest in the students' abilities, such as patients and clinical staff.

145. C: The median (middle) score is 86 because half (5) of the other scores are higher, and half (5) of the other scores are lower. The average score (all scores added together then divided by 11) is 82. It's important to calculate the mean and median scores. In this case, the very low score of 34 skewed the average score downward to 82, even though eight of the eleven students in the cohort scored higher than 82. If the low score were eliminated, the average of the other scores would be 86.8, near the median.

146. B: The nurse educator should establish a grading rubric that outlines exactly how many points will be awarded for several different criterion, such as grammar, clarity of thesis, and quality of evidence, as well as how many points will be removed, such as for late papers. The nurse should include the rubric with the syllabus and discuss the rubric with the class prior to assigning papers. The nurse educator should not depend on subjective grading criteria but should be as objective as possible.

147. D: Emotional intelligence is the ability to understand and perceive emotions in the self and others, helping the person to respond appropriately to others to avoid alienating people. This does not suggest that people have to be nice and smiling all of the time or freely expressing or suppressing emotions, but people with emotional intelligence are able to judge when it's appropriate to express or suppress emotions and can take action based on reasons appropriate to the situation at hand.

148. C: The average sentence length for college textbooks is about 25 words. Twenty-nine words or more are appropriate for graduate students but may be too complex for beginning college students. An average sentence length of 17 is appropriate for eighth to ninth grade, and sentence lengths of 11 words are appropriate for sixth grade. Because reading ability has decreased over the last decades, many textbooks are "watered down" and written at lower than a college reading level, so nurse educators should be aware of grade level when choosing texts.

149. D: The decline in the birth rate coupled with better healthcare and extended life expectancy is bringing about an aging of the population that will have a profound effect on nursing education, with more focus on the needs of the elderly. People will want and need more information about self-care and health maintenance. Nurses will need to focus more on degenerative diseases and other diseases associated with aging. Much nursing care will move out of the hospital and into the community.

150. A: The most important focus of patient education is self-care in terms of medical treatment and preventive medicine. Patients must learn to be independent in care because this in turn increases self-confidence and cost-effectiveness. Patients must be alert to changes in their condition and be able to carry out preventive measures to maintain health or improve health. Patients who are educated about health matters are more likely to remain compliant with medical treatment because they have a better understanding of the implications.

Nurse Educator Practice Test #2

1. The nurse educator has three years of experience and is beginning to feel confident when dealing with new situations but sometimes lacks flexibility and needs time to plan. According to Benner's stages of clinical competence, the nurse educator is in which stage?

a. Novice
b. Competent
c. Advanced beginner
d. Proficient

2. The school of nursing has found that students admitted with a grade point average (GPA) of C (2.0) in core prerequisite courses drop out of nursing school at a rate that is 30% higher than those with GPAs of A or B. What is the best solution to improve retention?

a. Raise GPA prerequisite requirements to A or B.
b. Inform applying students that a lower GPA places them at risk for dropping out.
c. Establish a policy that allows students receiving Cs in core courses to retake the courses to improve their grades.
d. Establish support courses to assist students with study skills.

3. With regards to the four-part condition-learner-performance-criterion method for writing behavioral objectives, which of the following is a well-written objective?

a. Using a mannequin, the student nurse will demonstrate the correct procedure for changing a sterile wound dressing.
b. After studying pain management, the student nurse will understand pain control.
c. After completing the dietary module on protein, the student nurse will understand what makes up a healthy diet.
d. After watching a demonstration of suctioning, the student nurse will list the reasons for suctioning.

4. The nurse educator is completing a learning contract with a student. Which of the following should be done initially?

a. Assess the learning needs and competencies of the student.
b. Identify learning objectives.
c. Define the roles of the student and the educator.
d. Identify resources for learning.

5. With regards to assessing the four types of readiness to learn, which type includes consideration of past coping mechanisms?

a. Emotional
b. Physical
c. Knowledge
d. Experiential

6. Which characteristic is typical of a field-dependent learner?

a. Easily affected and disturbed by criticism
b. Does not conform to peer pressure
c. Prefers learning by the lecture method
d. Provides self-directed goals

7. Which of the following teaching strategies is likely to be of the most value when teaching complex procedures that involve many steps?

a. Lecture
b. Debate
c. Algorithm
d. Concept mapping

8. The nurse educator is preparing a table of specifications prior to writing an exam (100 questions) for a pediatric unit regarding pain assessment and management. The approximate percentage of class time spent covering the content is indicated.

Content and % of time	**Recall (20%)**	**Understand (40%)**	**Apply (40%)**	**Total items**
Pathophysiology, chronic/acute (25%)	?	?	?	?
Behavioral response (10%)	2	4	4	10
Clinical manifestations (15%)	3	6	6	15
Cultural influences/barriers (10%)	2	4	4	10
Pain conditions (10%)	2	4	4	10
Diagnostic testing (5%)	1	2	2	5
Pain assessment (15%)	3	6	6	15
Medical and complementary management (10%)	2	4	4	10

When completing the table of specifications, what are the numbers for pathophysiology?

a. Recall, 2; understand, 4; apply, 4; total, 10
b. Recall, 3; understand, 6; apply, 6; total, 15
c. Recall, 5; understand, 5; apply, 15; total, 25
d. Recall, 5; understand, 10; apply, 10; total, 25

9. According to Carper's (1970) four patterns of knowing in nursing, which of the following refers to gaining knowledge through subjective means?

a. Empirics
b. Aesthetics
c. Personal knowledge
d. Moral knowledge

10. When planning group projects, which generational group could the nurse educator expect to be most likely to enjoy working in groups?

a. Baby boomers
b. Mature/silent generation
c. Generation Xers
d. Millennials

11. The nurse educator is coordinating an outreach program to attract minority students into the nursing program. Which of the following is the most essential component of the outreach program?

a. Minority role models
b. Financial advice
c. Guidance in application procedures
d. Outline of admission requirements

12. The nurse educator has a very diverse group of nursing students of various ages and is planning teaching approaches. What should he do to best meet the students' needs?

a. Ask students how they prefer to learn.
b. Conduct a learning styles inventory.
c. Observe the students in various types of activities.
d. Ask the advice of a more experienced nurse educator.

13. According to Kolb's Learning Style Inventory, which type of learning style does a person have if she likes to learn through a combination of concrete information and active experimentation and solves problems through trial and error?

a. Assimilative
b. Divergent
c. Accommodative
d. Convergent

14. When planning teaching approaches for students whose learning style preference is visual, which of the following actions of the nurse educator is most likely to be effective?

a. She provides written directions, illustrations, and videos of a procedure.
b. She explains a procedure while demonstrating and asks the students to repeat the steps to the procedure.
c. She provides hands-on experience.
d. She provides minimal explanation but lets the students explore equipment.

15. Which of the following is a violation of scholarly integrity?

a. A group of students studies together for a final exam.
b. Two students conducting separate research share information about sources.
c. A student who took a course the previous semester advises current students about what content to focus on for the final exam.
d. Two students doing a take-home test divide up the questions, and each do half of the work.

16. The school of nursing wants to attract a more diverse pool of competent nursing school applicants. Which type of screening requirements is most likely to produce the most diverse but competent pool?

a. Prerequisite course grade point average (GPA) of ≥B (3.0)
b. Multiple-criterion screening based on varying points for different criterion, including work experience, GPA of ≥ C (2.0) on prerequisites, academic and military backgrounds, and ≥62% on the Test of Essential Academic Skills (TEAS)
c. Prerequisite course GPA of ≥C and ≥62% on the TEAS
d. Lottery selection from all students who passed prerequisite courses with GPAs of ≥C

17. According to McCarthy's (1981) 4MAT system, which type of learner is most comfortable experimenting and manipulating?

a. Type 1: Imaginative
b. Type 2: Analytic
c. Type 3: Common sense
d. Type 4: Dynamic

18. According to William Perry's (1970) stages of cognitive and ethical development, the nurse educator should expect incoming freshman to be at which stage?

a. Dualism/received knowledge
b. Commitment/constructed knowledge
c. Relativism/procedural knowledge
d. Multiplicity/subjective Knowledge

19. According to the National League for Nursing, which of the following is the best description of the ideal educator-student relationship?

a. Authoritarian/prescriptive
b. Egalitarian/collaborative
c. Hierarchical/cooperative
d. Independent/dependent

20. The nurse educator is concerned about violating due process with a student who is failing a class and may be expelled from the nursing program. What information must she share with the student?

a. Problem, cost, and consequences
b. Problem, educator action, student action, and consequences
c. Problem, conditions, and consequences
d. Problem, solution, time frame, and consequences

21. A student who is on academic probation because of inadequate clinical performance states that she is very stressed because of the increased supervision and observation that is required, and this stress is interfering with her ability to concentrate. Which is the best solution for the nurse educator?

a. Meet with the student to counsel her about relaxation techniques.
b. Reduce the amount of supervision and observation.
c. Refer the student to a counselor.
d. Explain that the student has no other options.

22. A nursing student with mild cerebral palsy has slow, slightly slurred speech but has no cognitive impairment; however, during clinical rotations, some of the staff and patients have referred to her as mentally handicapped or retarded. What is the best solution for the nurse educator?

a. Tell staff and patients in advance that the student has cerebral palsy.
b. Take no action because the student must deal with this issue by herself.
c. Explain the issue to the student, and ask how she would like to deal with the problem.
d. Refer the issue to the ethics committee.

23. When a student with disabilities applies to enter the nursing program, which of the following issues are of the most concern?

a. Student qualifications and need for accommodations
b. Student age and cognitive ability
c. Accessibility and need for accommodations
d. Accessibility and student qualifications

24. A student has informed the nurse educator that he has dyslexia and has trouble taking adequate notes during lectures, so the educator provides him with printed notes and copies of slide show presentations. During a faculty meeting, another instructor, who is obviously unaware of the student's dyslexia, expresses concerns about his learning ability. What is the appropriate response of the nurse educator?

a. The nurse educator should tell the other instructor that the student has dyslexia.
b. The nurse educator should say nothing.
c. The nurse educator should suggest that the other instructor could talk to supportive services about the student.
d. The nurse educator should ask the student if he would consider discussing his dyslexia with the other instructors.

25. The nurse educator feels that there is a need for the university to develop an intervention program for nursing students who are impaired because of substance abuse. Which of the following is the primary consideration?

a. Educating students about the program
b. Ensuring confidentiality for the participants
c. Paying the costs of the program
d. Establishing the roles of those associated with the program

26. The state and institution in which the nursing educator practices do not require that nursing students disclose criminal backgrounds. What, if any, responsibility does the nurse educator have related to a student that she knows has a criminal background?

a. No responsibility
b. She should advise the student of state licensure restrictions for those with criminal backgrounds and about appeals procedures.
c. She should advise the nursing school to expel the student.
d. She should advise the student to get an attorney.

27. When the nurse educator is evaluating curricular design as part of program review, which four elements should be congruent?

a. Objectives, outcomes, subject matter, and learning activities
b. Mission, philosophy, data, and objectives
c. Objectives, goals, faculty, and students
d. Faculty, students, environment, and materials

28. According to Bevis's description of curricula, which type of curricula includes things that are taught but not evaluated, such as caring?

a. Operational
b. Hidden
c. Illegitimate
d. Null

29. The school of nursing is undergoing changes in its curricula. Which of the following is a barrier to curricular change?

a. Increased use of technology
b. Fear of loss of autonomy and control
c. Changes in healthcare
d. Increased need for home healthcare and community-based nursing care

30. Which of the following trends is likely to have the most impact on nursing education and curriculum development?

a. Aging of the population
b. Global violence
c. Globalization
d. Environmental challenges

31. Which theory of education has historically been the most common model for nursing schools, accrediting agencies, and state boards of nursing?

a. Humanism
b. Essentialism
c. Behaviorism
d. Progressivism

32. In the future of nursing, the nurse educator should expect that most advanced-practice nurses will enter the profession with which type of degree?

a. Associate degree
b. Baccalaureate degree
c. Master's degree
d. Doctorate

33. The nurse educator has completed a survey of six hospitals in the area of the university to determine the types of academic degrees the employed nurses have currently. The results are as follows:

- 60%: Associate of science in nursing (ASN) degree
- 5%: Diploma (registered nurse, RN)
- 10%: Licensed vocational nurse (LVN)
- 20%: Baccalaureate (bachelor of science in nursing, BSN) degree
- 4%: Master's (master of science in nursing, MSN) degree
- 1%: Doctorate

The university is considering creating a bridge program to provide educational mobility options. Based on these findings, which type of bridge program is most likely to best serve the needs of the local institutions and to be cost-effective for the university?

a. LVN to ASN
b. ASN to BSN
c. MSN to doctorate
d. BSN to MSN

34. The nursing program in which the nurse educator is employed groups content according to specific practice settings and content areas, but the nurse educator has proposed the integration of core concepts throughout the curricula. Which of the following concepts would best lend itself to integration as an initial trial?

a. Pain
b. Critical care
c. Home health
d. Elimination

35. Who is primarily responsible for a student's learning?

a. The student
b. The instructor
c. The program
d. The state board of nursing

36. In a master's degree program for advanced-practice nursing, which of the following has the most influence over content?

a. State board of nursing
b. Certifying agency
c. Accrediting agency
d. Program director

37. If the nurse educator is interested in building the curriculum around the concept of self-care, whose theory would be used as a framework?

a. Watson
b. Nightingale
c. Orem
d. Maslow

38. The school of nursing is undergoing curriculum revision and is changing from the use of a theory of nursing as a conceptual framework to a more nontraditional framework, the KSVME framework (Webber, 2002). The conceptual cornerstones of the framework include the following:

K—nursing knowledge
S—nursing skills
V—nursing values
M—nursing meanings
E—?

What does the *E* in the model refer to?

a. Nursing evaluation
b. Nursing equality
c. Nursing education
d. Nursing experience

39. The nurse educator is designing curriculum and has determined that the ability to think critically is a desired outcome. What is the next step?

a. Define critical thinking.
b. Establish a time frame.
c. Identify competencies.
d. Identify assessment methods.

40. Which of the following is an example of passive learning?

a. The student takes notes while listening to the instructor give a lecture.
b. The student participates in a group activity.
c. The student prepares a slide show presentation about a topic.
d. The student prepares a video demonstrating a procedure.

41. The nurse educator wants to include structured and unstructured learning activities for students in class. Which of the following is an example of an unstructured learning activity?

a. Students are assigned a topic and must present a report to the class.
b. Students are assigned a reading and must complete a worksheet.
c. Students must study a prescribed text and write a summary.
d. Students must attend a community meeting to observe the types of activities/interactions that occur and report back to the class.

42. According to Bloom's original taxonomy (1956), in the cognitive domain, which of the following represents the lowest order of learning?

a. Comprehension
b. Knowledge
c. Application
d. Analysis

43. Which of the following activities is most likely to enhance development of the affective domain of learning (Bloom)?

a. Lecture
b. Small-group activities
c. Concept mapping
d. Storytelling

44. A nurse educator who mentors junior faculty and reads extensively in other fields of study is demonstrating which type of scholarship?

a. Integration
b. Application
c. Teaching
d. Discovery

45. According to Dave's taxonomy regarding the psychomotor domain of learning, which of the following levels is a student demonstrating if he is able to carry out an action in a logical order with just a few noncritical errors, has good coordination of movements, and needs variable amounts of time to complete the action?

a. Naturalization
b. Manipulation
c. Imitation
d. Precision

46. The nurse educator has received student evaluations, which showed that students think that her class presentations are boring and hard to follow, but she doesn't understand what the specific problem is. Which of the following is probably the best method to identify and rectify the problem?

a. Videotape class presentations and lectures.
b. Ask students during class to explain the problem.
c. Ask a colleague to attend classes and evaluate the presentations.
d. Ask a few students outside of class to explain the problem.

47. The novice nurse educator has overestimated the students' knowledge and abilities and assigned an activity that is much too difficult, so many of them are unable to complete the assignment and are confused about using the equipment. Which type of learning constraint does this represent?

a. Faculty constraint
b. Student constraint
c. Time constraint
d. Resource constraint

48. Which of the following is an appropriate use of a summative evaluation?

a. Assess learning activities during development and use.
b. Assess problems that arise during implementation.
c. Assess the ability of students to apply knowledge.
d. Assess students' learning outcomes.

49. According to Bevis's (1988) six types of learning, a student who is able to gain insight by recognizing patterns and relationships is engaging in which type of learning?

a. Directive
b. Rational
c. Syntactic
d. Inquiry

50. A community near the nursing school experienced a severe tornado, leaving many people injured and homeless. The nurse educator wants to use this situation as an opportunity to help students understand the needs of the community after a disaster through service learning. Which of the following is the best example of service learning?

a. The students study about illnesses and injuries common to disasters, such as tornadoes.
b. The students go into the community to survey the health needs of those affected by the tornado.
c. The students assist in giving tetanus injections to the injured at a hospital clinic.
d. The students use data regarding injuries to create a map of injury severity along the path of the tornado.

51. The nurse educator is concerned with helping students develop their long-term memories. Which is the best strategy for teaching how to store information in long-term memory?

a. Limit the amount of information to five to nine items at one time.
b. Link new information to already-learned information.
c. Tell students to review the information daily.
d. Provide information in 20-minute blocks of time.

52. According to Ausubel and Robinson's (1969) and Ausubel's (1978) assimilation theory, which of the following is the most critical factor in student learning?

a. Motivation
b. Memorization
c. Prior knowledge
d. Attention span

53. If a nurse educator is using Knowles' model of adult learning as a guide to teaching, how will she plan the course content and teaching strategies?

a. Using a strict, prescribed model
b. Independently
c. Collaboratively with experts
d. Collaboratively with students

54. Which approach to learning places the most emphasis on the affective domain?

a. Behaviorism
b. Humanism
c. Critical pedagogy
d. Feminist pedagogy

55. The nurse educator has assigned group projects, but one group reports that a member of the group has been uncooperative, has missed group meetings, and is discourteous to other members of the group. What is the role of the nurse educator?

a. He should allow the group to resolve the issue.
b. He should counsel the group about how to deal with the difficult group member.
c. He should reassign the difficult group member to a different group.
d. He should meet with the difficult group member and discuss how the member's behavior is affecting learning.

56. The nurse educator receives a research paper from a student and recognizes the paper as one that was written by another student in the previous year. Because the educator kept a copy of the original paper, he has definitive proof of plagiarism. What is the best approach to dealing with the student's violation of the code of conduct?

a. Check administrative policies regarding violations, and follow protocol.
b. Refer the student to the dean.
c. Fail the student.
d. Talk with the student about the reasons for the violation.

57. The nurse educator is designing cooperative learning assignments in which students will work in groups. When forming groups, what is the ideal size for small-group work?

a. 2–3 students
b. 3–5 students
c. 5–7 students
d. 7–10 students

58. Which of the following activities is best for reinforcing knowledge as opposed to introducing new information?

a. Demonstration
b. Cooperative learning
c. An algorithm
d. Games

59. The nursing program is transitioning to problem-based learning. What should the nurse educator expect in relation to workload?

a. Workload will decrease because education is more student-centered.
b. Workload should vary little from other types of learning.
c. Workload will probably increase significantly during the development stage.
d. Workload will decrease markedly after the development stage.

60. The nurse educator has administered a classroom assessment technique (CAT) at the conclusion of a series of classes about intravenous therapy, which included simulation practice, asking students to indicate their level of confidence in a number of items related to intravenous (IV) therapy. The results for 30 students were as follows:

ITEM	None	Low	Medium	High
Locating veins	—	—	5	25
Conducting skin prep	—	—	2	28
Starting IV with needle	1	7	17	5
Starting IV with catheter	3	10	14	3
Calculating drop rate	1	11	14	4
Evaluating IV site	—	—	4	26

Based on the results of the CAT, which action is most appropriate for the nurse educator?

a. Proceed to the next lesson because these results are within normal limits.
b. Incorporate practice starting IVs and calculating drop rates into the next lessons.
c. Repeat the entire series of classes about IV therapy.
d. Conduct further testing to determine the students' abilities to start IVs.

61. The nurse educator has a number of multicultural/English as a second language (ESL) students in class and notes that some are reluctant to answer questions or don't respond when asked a question. What wait time should he use after asking a student a question before giving a second prompt?

a. 2–3 seconds
b. 4–6 seconds
c. 7–9 seconds
d. 10–12 seconds

62. Which of the following is the first step to helping students develop cultural awareness?

a. Assess students' perception of themselves and others.
b. Provide factual information about other cultures.
c. Plan activities that expose students to different perspectives.
d. Encourage personal exchanges among different cultures.

63. The nurse educator is assigning students to clinical learning environments, but the supervisor on one unit has been openly hostile to students, causing many students to leave the unit in tears and others to beg to be reassigned. Intervention has not changed the supervisor's attitude; she is equally harsh with her staff, and the director of nursing refuses to take action. What is the best solution for the nurse educator?

a. Stop assigning students to this unit.
b. Assign students in pairs consisting of one novice with one more experienced student.
c. Teach coping skills to help students deal with the supervisor.
d. Assign only the top students to the unit.

64. Because of an outbreak of norovirus, one unit at the hospital has closed temporarily, so the number of patients available for student clinical assignments has decreased. Which of the following is the best option for the clinical nurse educator?

a. Delay clinical practice until the unit reopens.
b. Assign students for half the normal time, and rotate groups.
c. Use the dual- or multiple-assignment strategy.
d. Locate another site for clinical practice.

65. According to Alevi et al.'s (1991) psychomotor skill categorization, comprising "fundamental," "general therapeutic and diagnostic," and "specialized therapeutic and diagnostic," which of the following skills is categorized as "general therapeutic and diagnostic"?

a. Range-of-motion exercises
b. Palpation and percussion
c. Hand-washing techniques
d. Tracheostomy suctioning

66. The nurse educator plans to use a simulated or standardized patient in the learning resource center. Which of the following is the best use of the simulated or standardized patient?

a. Enema practice
b. IV therapy practice
c. Physical examination practice
d. CPR practice

67. The nurse educator is presenting information on a screen with videos and still photos projected but with verbal introductions to the screened material interspersed throughout the presentation. What are the best positions for the screen and the educator?

a. Screen to one side and educator in the center, with his body turned toward the screen
b. Screen in the center and educator to one side, with his body turned toward the screen
c. Screen to one side and educator in the center, with his body facing the audience
d. Screen to the center and educator to one side, with his body facing the audience

68. The nurse educator is giving a lecture with a slide show presentation that is projected on a 60-inch-wide screen. For ease of viewing, what is the furthest distance a viewer should sit away from the projected images?

a. 30 feet
b. 50 feet
c. 20 feet
d. 10 feet

69. The primary purpose of evaluation in nursing education is to do which of the following?

a. Identify problems.
b. Facilitate learning.
c. Judge teaching effectiveness.
d. Make decisions or assign grades.

70. Which of the following is the first step to conducting an evaluation?

a. Determining the purpose
b. Selecting evaluators
c. Selecting an evaluation design
d. Identifying the time frame

71. Which of the following decision models is most appropriate to measure the strengths and weaknesses of a program, to identify needs of a target population, and to identify options?

a. Logic model
b. Context-input-process-product (CIPP) model
c. Assessment model
d. Benchmarking

72. Which of the following evaluation instruments is the most efficient to use if the nurse educator wants to evaluate the attitudes of students about a particular topic, such as multiculturalism?

a. Questionnaire
b. Interview
c. Observation
d. Likert scale

73. Two nurse educators administer the same evaluation instrument to one set of students, but they get markedly different results. What type of problem does this suggest?

a. Reliability
b. Measurement
c. Validity
d. Comprehension

74. The nurse educator is conducting student evaluations. Which of the following is true regarding norm-referenced interpretation of data?

a. Students are compared and ranked, with one at the highest level and one at the lowest level.
b. Students are compared to preset criteria to determine competency.
c. Students are compared to themselves over time.
d. Student results are used to establish norms or benchmarks.

75. The nurse educator is surprised to find that a student who excelled in the classroom and learning resource center seems completely disorganized and unprepared for caring for patients during clinical practice. What is her best approach?

a. Advise the student that his clinical performance is not adequate.
b. Place him on academic probation.
c. Describe observations and discuss with the student.
d. Refer him to a counselor.

76. As part of a discussion about Alzheimer's disease, the nurse educator plans to show video clips from documentaries and movies depicting patients with dementia. What is the optimal maximum length of time for a video clip?

a. 2–3 minutes
b. 4–6 minutes
c. 7–9 minutes
d. 10–15 minutes

77. The nurse educator is considering videotaping students performing specific tasks in the lab so the student and educator can review the videotapes together. Which of the following is the primary disadvantage of videotaping students?

a. Students may feel nervous or threatened.
b. Videotaping is time-consuming.
c. Videotaping requires the consent of the students.
d. Videotaping is a complex procedure.

78. The nurse educator has asked students to do a concept map of a patient's care plan but finds that some students have considerable difficulty creating the concept map, whereas others find it very easy. Which type of learner is most likely to do well creating concept maps?

a. Visual
b. Kinesthetic
c. Auditory
d. Mixed

79. A student is struggling with classroom content and clinical practice and may fail the nurse educator's course unless her competency improves. Which is the best course of action for the nurse educator?

a. Place the student on probation.
b. Warn her about possible course failure.
c. Collaborate with her to establish a learning contract.
d. Refer her to the director of the nursing program.

80. The nurse educator is constructing a test that includes interpretive items—paragraphs or graphs about which the student must answer questions. Which type of question is the best for interpretive items?

a. Essay/narrative
b. Short-answer or multiple-choice
c. Matching
d. True-false questions

81. When writing tests to evaluate students, which type of question is the weakest?

a. Essay/narrative
b. Short-answer
c. Multiple-choice
d. True-false

82. Which of the following is the best measure of variability when assessing test scores?

a. Standard deviation
b. Normal curve
c. Median
d. Range

83. When using Chen's (1990) theory-driven program evaluation and conducting normative treatment evaluation of the nursing-school program, "treatment" refers to which of the following?

a. Administrative procedures
b. Student activities
c. Curriculum and teaching strategies
d. Faculty structure

84. When conducting program evaluation, which of the following is the best method to determine if there is faculty consensus regarding the mission and philosophy of the school of nursing?

a. Brainstorming
b. Content map
c. Thematic analysis
d. Delphi technique

85. Which of the following is likely to provide the best qualitative evaluation of teaching strategies and teaching effectiveness?

a. Focus group
b. Internally developed evaluation
c. Peer review
d. Self-evaluation

86. What was the purpose of the 5 Million Lives Campaign (2006 to 2008) of the Institute for Healthcare Improvement?

a. Promote delivery of culturally competent care.
b. Promote patient teaching and education.
c. Increase access to preventive medicine.
d. Reduce incidents of medical harm that occur in hospitals.

87. Which of the following may be categorized as a hidden cost of a nurse educator program?

a. Faculty salaries
b. Orientation program
c. Faculty absenteeism and low productivity
d. Heating and air-conditioning

88. The nurse educator has been contracted to develop a number of patient education courses, such as "Managing Diabetic Care," for which the hospital will charge insurance companies or patients directly. This is an example of which of the following?

a. Cost benefit
b. Cost recovery
c. Cost savings
d. Cost containment

89. According to the information-processing model of memory, what occurs during the first stage of memory?

a. Paying attention
b. Memory storage
c. Processing
d. Action

90. Which of the following is a central concept of Bandura's (1977, 2001) social learning theory?

a. Stimulus-response
b. Information processing
c. Perception
d. Role modeling

91. According to the psychodynamic learning theory, which ego defense mechanism is a student using when she expresses or behaves the opposite of what she feels in response to a perceived threat?

a. Displacement
b. Reaction formation
c. Projection
d. Sublimation

92. For which three determinants of learning should the nurse educator assess students?

a. Motivation, cognition, and perseverance
b. Attention, motivation, and learning style
c. Needs, readiness, and learning style
d. Attitude, motivation, and learning style

93. When writing objectives, which one of the following verbs should the nurse educator avoid because the meaning may be ambiguous or unclear?

a. Apply
b. Choose
c. Demonstrate
d. Understand

94. The nurse educator is planning a lecture and discussion and plans to use a slide show presentation to highlight important points. What is the maximum number of words he should use per slide?

a. 10
b. 25
c. 50
d. 100

95. The nurse educator is planning to teach students to use an IV infusion pump, but the pump in the lab is an older model with different settings than the ones used in the hospital. Which of the following is the best solution?

a. Use the older model for practice, but show a video of the newer model.
b. Use the older model for practice because the principles are basically the same.
c. Replace the older model with a newer one to match those in use currently.
d. Show a video of the newer model, and ask students to explain rather than demonstrate the procedures.

96. The nurse educator would like the nursing program to purchase a number of high-fidelity, whole-body simulators for the nursing resource center. From a program perspective, what is the primary disadvantage?

a. Extended learning curve
b. High risk of injury
c. High cost
d. Student resistance

97. Which of the following teaching methods by the nurse educator requires an active learner role?

a. Role-modeling
b. Demonstration
c. Lecture
d. One-on-one instruction

98. Which of the following teaching methods is best to help students learn affective skills?

a. Lecture
b. Role-playing
c. Simulation
d. Demonstration

99. When considering the purchase of instructional materials, what are the three major components of instructional materials that the nurse educator should evaluate?

a. Delivery system, content, and presentation
b. Learner, media, and task
c. Realia, illusionary representation, and symbolic representation
d. Written, demonstration, and audiovisual

100. Based on evidence-based research into information retention, which mode of learning does the nurse educator expect will result in the lowest rate of retention?

a. Looking at posters, slides, or pictures
b. Reading a textbook
c. Watching a videotape or DVD presentation
d. Practicing with models or real equipment

101. As a class project, the nurse educator's students are creating educational materials for oncology patients. For which grade level (first to college) should she advise the students to prepare written materials?

a. Second grade
b. Fifth grade
c. Eighth grade
d. Twelfth grade

102. According to Gardner's (1988, 1999) theory of multiple intelligences, a student whose intelligence profile is strongly naturalist would do best with which of the following learning activities?

a. Conducting interviews and discussing case studies
b. Reviewing charts, graphs, illustrations, and maps
c. Listening to and classifying heart sounds
d. Creating an artistic project (a painting or video)

103. The nurse educator is designing an online course about nursing ethics and would like to include a chapter from a commercial textbook on the same topic. What must he do to ensure that there is no violation of copyright laws?

a. No action is necessary because this use is within fair-use guidelines.
b. Because of possible fair-use violations, the instructor should get permission from the publisher of the book.
c. He should notify the publisher of his fair use of the material.
d. He should determine whether less than 25% of the book will be used.

104. When designing an online course, the nurse educator is concerned that there is a balance between an asynchronous and synchronous learning space. Which of the following activities would be the best presented asynchronously?

a. Instructor office hours
b. Whiteboard drawings
c. Chat
d. Video viewing

105. When planning a simulation exercise for students, which level of fidelity is the nurse educator concerned with when trying to ensure that the simulation represents reality in a believable manner?

a. Technological
b. Equipment
c. Environmental
d. Psychological

106. The school of nursing has received a state grant to cover the costs of equipment and renovation in order to develop a simulation lab with two high-fidelity, whole-body simulators separated by a walled-in computer station in the middle, with one-way glass windows so that the instructors can view the students and control the simulations. What is likely to pose the biggest challenge?

a. Student acceptance
b. Faculty training
c. Maintenance costs
d. Interdepartmental envy

107. The nurse educator is evaluating the results of a 20-question exam that was administered to the class and finds the following item difficulties (*p* values) for individual questions:

0	0.1	0.2	0.3	0.4	0.5	0.6	0.7	0.8	0.9	1
—	8	1	13, 18	14	6, 19	7, 15	4, 5, 9, 16	3, 10, 17, 20	2, 11	12

Based on these *p* values, what conclusion can she make about the probable difficulty of the test?

a. The difficulty level is probably appropriate for the class.
b. The difficulty level is probably too low for the class.
c. The difficulty level is probably too high for the class.
d. The data are inadequate to make conclusions.

108. When analyzing the answers on a multiple-choice test, the nurse educator finds that the point biserial index (PBI) for most items ranged from 0.1 to 0.2. What does this indicate?

a. The items should be revised.
b. The items are acceptable but could be improved.
c. The items should be rejected.
d. The items are excellent.

109. As part of a student's clinical evaluation, the nurse educator will observe the student doing a dressing change and provide feedback. What should he do initially as part of the feedback process?

a. Tell the student when he is beginning the process.
b. Ask the student to do a self-evaluation.
c. Outline expectations.
d. Describe observations.

110. How frequently should program evaluation be carried out?

a. Continuously
b. Annually
c. Biannually
d. Every five years

111. The nurse educator is employed at a baccalaureate school of nursing that is applying for accreditation with the Commission on Collegiate Nursing Education (CCNE). What is the initial term of accreditation for institutions applying to CCNE for accreditation?

a. Up to 2 years
b. Up to 3 years
c. Up to 5 years
d. Up to 10 years

112. The school of nursing is using a fourth-generation qualitative method-oriented program assessment. The nurse educator should be aware that which of the following may not receive adequate assessment with this method?

a. Stakeholders' viewpoints
b. Outcomes
c. Program strengths
d. Program weaknesses

113. In Chen's (1990) theory-driven program evaluation, in the *implementation environment* part of the evaluation, which dimension includes the effects of the immediate environment (campus housing, student services)?

a. Interorganizational relationship
b. Implementing organization
c. Macrocontext
d. Microcontext

114. As part of program evaluation, the nurse educator is chairperson of the ad hoc committee charged with evaluating interorganizational relationships. Which of the following is the most appropriate evaluation technique to help complete this task?

a. Survey local hospitals and organizations that hire graduate nurses to determine their level of satisfaction.
b. Study relevant issues in healthcare related to the local area and state.
c. Survey the faculty and ask about interorganizational relationships.
d. Draw a concept map showing interorganizational relationships.

115. Which of the following is a quantitative technique for assessment of student outcomes?

a. Written examination
b. Self-assessment
c. Rating scale
d. Observation

116. Which of the following suggests the possible need for revision of the nursing program's mission and philosophy statements?

a. The mission and philosophy statements are congruent with those of the university.
b. The nursing program fact sheet does not include the mission and philosophy statements.
c. Many faculty members disagree with the mission and philosophy statements.
d. Many students are unable to articulate the mission and philosophy of the nursing school.

117. The principle of *linear congruence* refers to which of the following?

a. Administrative hierarchy
b. Grading policy
c. Mathematical processes
d. Course sequencing

118. Which of the following probably provides the best measure of student performance?

a. Multiple-choice question exam
b. Essay exam
c. Clinical simulation testing
d. Research paper

119. Which qualification is advised for nurse educators teaching in graduate programs for advance practice nurses?

a. Doctor of nursing practice (DNP) or terminal degree in area of related specialty
b. DNP
c. MSN
d. BSN or MSN

120. In order to meet the requirements for professional scholarship, the nurse educator has elected to focus on the scholarship of discovery. Which of the following activities would be appropriate?

a. She reads extensively in the fields of health prevention and healthcare policy and produces an annotated bibliography.
b. She assigns groups of students to different types of simulations and evaluates short-term and long-term retention of skills, producing a research paper and publishing it in a juried journal.
c. She starts a mentoring program for novice faculty and serves as a mentor in the program.
d. She works with a local hospital and community agency to develop a free clinic for low-income and uninsured community members.

121. The novice nurse educator is adept at programming simulations and has been assisting more experienced but less computer-literate faculty with programming, but this is taking considerably more time than the nurse educator had planned because of the number of requests for help. Which of the following is the best solution?

a. Tell other educators that they must do their own programming.
b. Set aside a specified period of time each week to assist others.
c. Offer to provide training classes for other educators.
d. Complain to the director of the program.

122. The nurse educator works in a community college associate degree program that has a partnership with a local community hospital, where students complete clinical practice, and she wants to use this partnership to develop service-learning opportunities for the students. Which of the following hospital activities presents the best opportunity for service learning?

a. The hospital conducts health and blood pressure screenings at local senior citizens' groups and retirement communities.
b. The hospital conducts classes for community members at the hospital about various health topics.
c. The hospital provides podcasts about various health topics for health consumers.
d. The hospital is represented at a booth at an annual job fair at the community college.

123. The nurse educator wants to get more information about community health needs as part of program planning and plans to conduct a survey. Which of the following may be the best source of information?

a. Hospital administration
b. Local physicians
c. Local service agencies (Salvation Army, Red Cross)
d. County public health department

124. The nurse educator is concerned about the impact that a newly proposed state legislation may have on the financing of nursing education, and she makes an appointment with a state legislator to discuss the issue. Which professional role is she exercising?

a. Change leader
b. Advocate
c. Researcher
d. Collaborator

125. The nurse educator is concerned because the university has cut funding to the nursing program by 10% but left other programs with financing intact, even though enrollment is growing in nursing and declining in some of the other programs. Which of the following is his best course of action?

a. Begin an Internet petition to ask the university to reinstate funding to the nursing program.
b. Contact the state board of education and state board of nursing regarding the problem.
c. Write letters about the issue to local and regional newspapers.
d. Organize the nursing faculty and conduct research about enrollment trends and return on investment to present to the university administration.

126. The nurse educator is taking classes, serving on committees, volunteering in the community, and serving as a mentor in addition to teaching responsibilities, and she is feeling overwhelmed. Which of the following is the best action she could take to resolve this issue?

a. Stop all activities except those directly related to teaching.
b. Prioritize and refocus energies.
c. Discuss the problem with the head of the department.
d. Seek counseling to help cope with responsibilities.

127. Which activity by the nurse educator best demonstrates a strategy for change?

a. He proposes a committee to evaluate the need for process revision.
b. He applies to a DNP program.
c. He volunteers at a free clinic two days per month.
d. He conducts item analysis of an examination used in class.

128. The nurse educator wants to review the best evidence, positive and negative, regarding healthcare interventions. Which of the following will likely provide the best information for evidence-based practice?

a. Cochrane Review
b. WebMD
c. MedlinePlus
d. Healthcare Cost and Utilization Project (HCUP)

129. The nurse educator is designing qualitative research to determine the attitudes of the faculty toward changes in the nursing program. Which of the following poses the most likely problem with qualitative research?

a. Time constraints
b. Participation
c. Bias
d. Costs

130. The nursing school has established 90% as the National Council Licensure Examination (NCLEX) pass rate, based on past performance and a substantial number of high-risk students; however, the actual pass rate is 82%. Which initial action is most indicated?

a. Establish higher admission standards.
b. Establish academic support classes especially for nursing students.
c. Conduct a curricular review to establish the need for curricular revision.
d. Review NCLEX group performance data and curricular information data.

131. The nurse educator is supervising a student in clinical practice at the hospital while the student prepares to change a patient's dressing for the first time. The student is very nervous and states that she can't remember the steps to the procedure. What is the best response of the nurse educator?

a. Tell the student, "It will come to you. Just relax."
b. Ask the student, "What would help you feel more comfortable doing this procedure?"
c. Change the assignment so the student doesn't have to do the procedure.
d. Tell the student, "Don't worry. I'll be right here helping you."

132. The nurse educator is providing advice about research to a group of students who are researching grief related to the death of a spouse. At this stage of their research, 95% of the participants are female. What type of bias does this indicate?

a. Androcentricity
b. Sexism
c. Gender insensitivity
d. Familism

133. According to Noddings' four principles of caring education, which of the following promotes confirmation?

a. The nurse educator allows time at the end of class for students to provide evaluations.
b. The nurse tells students about personal values and goals.
c. The nurse educator plans many opportunities to provide constructive criticism and formative feedback to students.
d. The nurse educator ensures that all students have access to the same resources.

134. Which of the following is the best example of reflective practice?

a. The nurse educator plans for the following semester.
b. The nurse educator serves on the program review committee.
c. The nurse educator recognizes the need for program change.
d. The nurse educator meets with a group of students after class ends to discuss their learning experience.

135. Which of the following is the primary purpose of creating a curriculum matrix as part of curricular design?

a. To organize knowledge and provide a coherent curriculum based on a chosen model
b. To provide an organized method of curriculum evaluation
c. To provide a means of visualizing the course content and sequencing
d. To ensure that curriculum is evidence-based

136. The nurse educator is serving on the curricular revision committee. The most important factor in gaining cooperation of other faculty members with the process of curricular revision is which of the following?

a. Provide updates of information about revision regularly.
b. Clearly outline the need for curricular revision.
c. Explain the consequences of failure to carry out curricular revision.
d. Actively involve all faculty members.

137. Which of the following is the best approach to preparing students to pass the NCLEX exam?

a. Teach to the test.
b. Provide students a thorough nursing education.
c. Advise students to do NCLEX practice exams.
d. Include NCLEX preparation manuals in course work.

138. Which of the following federal laws protects the privacy of student educational records and reports?

a. FERPA
b. HIPAA
c. ADA
d. IDEA

139. Which of the following is an inappropriate exercise in academic freedom on the part of the nurse educator?

a. She establishes grading practices for her class that are different from those of other instructors.
b. She advises the students that some of the rules of the university are outdated and tells the students to ignore them.
c. She tells students that they should write a petition to the administration if they are unhappy with the rules.
d. She tells students that religious beliefs have a place in health science.

140. According to the four Cs of curriculum development (commitment, compatibility, communication, and contribution), compatibility refers to which of the following?

a. Willingness to expend the necessary time, energy, and resources
b. Willingness to focus attention on common needs and curriculum as a whole rather than on individual courses
c. Requirements include facilitator, gatekeeper, harmonizer, and housekeeper.
d. Requirements include consensus, negotiation, and compromise.

141. The Classroom Organization and Management Program (COMP) (Evertson and Harris, 1995, 1999) focuses on which of the following as a means for the nurse educator to communicate expectations?

a. Authority and respect
b. Standards and ethics
c. Assignments and outcomes
d. Rules and procedures

142. The nurse educator is concerned about a student's ineffective clinical behavior and wants to help her develop her emotional intelligence. Which of the following is likely to be most effective?

a. Assign readings about emotional intelligence.
b. Model appropriate emotional behavior.
c. Assign a reflective journal for the student to explore her feelings and emotions.
d. Describe appropriate behavior in terms of emotional reactions and responses.

143. The nurse educator is concerned that some students lack adequate reading comprehension strategies and is conducting a workshop about reading skills, focusing on the SQ3R method. Which of the following should he stress that the students do first?

a. Survey
b. Summarize
c. Search
d. Select

144. The nurse educator allows students much autonomy in class and provides little guidance or classroom management. Which classroom management style does this most typify?

a. Indulgent
b. Authoritarian
c. Authoritative
d. Permissive

145. Which of the following models of clinical education is likely to provide the most benefit to a senior or graduate nursing student?

a. Clinical teaching partnership
b. Paired model
c. Preceptorship
d. One student—one patient

146. Which of the following student behaviors reflects a humanistic perspective on motivation?

a. Motivation relates to a positive association with the instructor.
b. Motivation relates to the need to associate with peers and connect with others.
c. Motivation relates to thoughts and beliefs.
d. Motivation relates to personal need for growth.

147. The nurse educator is the chairperson for the committee planning a new learning resource center. The rules and regulations of which of the following governmental agencies are the most important to consider?

a. ADA
b. OSHA
c. CDC
d. CMS

148. The nurse educator is planning learning experiences to help students develop critical thinking skills. What is her first step?

a. Decide on the learning outcomes.
b. Select a teaching strategy.
c. Create an anticipatory set.
d. Design evaluation measures.

149. The nurse educator makes an effort to know what is going on in the classroom at all times and to ensure that the students feel safe and comfortable. According to Kounin, this is an example of which of the following?

a. Accountability
b. The ripple effect
c. Withitness
d. Overlapping

150. The nurse educator is teaching a distance-learning course via the Internet and wants to encourage student interaction and a sense of class unity. Which of the following first assignments is best?

a. Ask the students to write a summary of the first chapter, and ask them to comment on at least two other students' summaries.
b. Ask students to write a brief biography, compile them into one file without students' names, and post for students to read.
c. Ask the students to write about why they are taking the class and post for students to read.
d. Ask the students to write a brief biography to share with other students, explaining their reasons for taking the class, and ask them to comment on at least two other students' biographies.

Answers and Explanations

1. B: Benner's stages of clinical competence are listed as follows:

- Novice: minimal experience and governed by rules and learned behavior; not adaptable
- Advanced beginner: beginning to gain experience and has improved coping
- Competent: has two to three years of experience and is coping well and dealing with new experiences but is not flexible and requires extra time for planning
- Proficient: has a holistic view and can draw from experience; is more adaptable and able to make decisions based on knowledge and principles
- Expert: provides excellent intuitive care based on extensive experience

2. D: The easiest solution would be to raise the required GPA, but this would eliminate a large group of students and impact diversity, so the best solution would be to establish support courses to assist students with study skills. Many students with lower GPAs have poor strategies for studying and have poor test-taking skills, and some may have learning disabilities, so they should be assessed for learning disabilities as part of the support courses.

3. A: Using a mannequin (condition), the student nurse (learner) will demonstrate (performance) the correct procedure for changing a sterile wound dressing (criterion). Behavioral objectives comprise:

- Condition: This is the testing situation and may include resources, assistance, or constraints.
- Learner: This is the person who is going to carry out the task.
- Performance: This is the action, which may be seen (write, list, suction, change) or unseen (recall, identify).
- Criterion: This should, as specifically as possible, describe in qualitative or quantitative measures how the behavior should be performed.

4. B: The initial step to a learning contract is to identify learning objectives, with the educator encouraging the student to self-identify. Then, the educator should review the process of a learning contract with the student. The educator should provide the student with information about learning resources, such as books, Web sites, and audiovisual tools and should assess the student's learning needs and competencies. The educator must clearly define roles and help to plan the learning process in collaboration with the student, negotiating the time frame. After implementation, some renegotiation may be necessary, and all progress should be documented.

5. D: The four types of readiness to learn include the following:

- Experiential: past coping mechanisms, cultural background, locus of control, orientation, and aspiration level
- Emotional: level of anxiety, support system, motivation, risky behavior, frame of mind, and stage of development
- Physical: measures of ability, task complexity, environmental effects, status of health, and gender
- Knowledge: current knowledge base, cognitive abilities, learning disabilities, and learning style

6. A: A field-dependent learner is easily affected and disturbed by criticism, conforms to peer pressure, is influenced by feedback, likes material to be organized, orients socially to the world, likes facts, wants learning relevant to personal experience, needs external goals and reinforcement, and prefers discussion to lecture. A field-independent learner is unaffected by criticism, doesn't conform to peer pressure, is not really influenced by feedback, likes to organize own material, orients impersonally to the world, likes applying principles, enjoys new ideas and concepts, is self-directed, and prefers lectures to discussion.

7. C: Algorithms are especially useful teaching strategies when teaching complex procedures that involve many steps. Algorithms involve breaking tasks into yes/no steps, helping students to identify critical information for problem-solving, and helping them to develop problem-solving skills. However, developing an algorithm is time-consuming—up to six or eight hours at times—and requires that the educator define the steps clearly. Algorithms do reduce the amount of one-on-one time or lecture time that the instructor needs to spend with students.

8. D: The table of specifications is completed to ensure that the number of test questions corresponds to the percentage of time the material was covered in the class or readings and is weighted according to the target skill. Because pathophysiology, chronic/acute comprised approximately 25% of the content, then 25% of the questions (25 out of 100) should be focused on this area, with 20% (5) for recall, 40% (10) for understanding, and 40% (10) for application.

Content and %	Recall (20%)	Understand (40%)	Apply (40%)	Total items
Pathophysiology, chronic/acute (25%)	5	10	10	25

9. B: Carper's (1970) four patterns of knowing in nursing include the following:

- Empirics: focuses on facts, theories, and laws and the science of nursing; generally referred to as empirical knowledge
- Aesthetics: focuses on knowledge gained through subjective means as well as subjective expression
- Personal knowledge: focuses on the interactions and transactions that occur between the nurse and the patient
- Moral knowledge: focuses on application of norms and ethical codes to real situations more than just by studying them

10. D: Millennials (born in the years 1981 to 2003) tend to be team players and enjoy working in groups. They tend to accept authority and follow rules but like to balance work and personal time. They are often outspoken, optimistic, and self-confident. Millennials grew up with technology and feel comfortable with technological approaches to learning. They are commonly involved in service activities and are socially aware. Because more than one-third of millennials are non-white or Hispanic, they are a diverse group.

11. A: Although financial advice, admission requirements, and application guidance are all useful, an essential component of an outreach program to attract minority students into the nursing profession is the availability of minority role models. Minority students need to see and interact with nurses with whom they share a common background so they can relate and feel more comfortable asking questions. Minority students may often feel quite isolated in nursing programs, and minority role models may also serve as mentors after students are admitted.

12. B: The nurse educator should begin by conducting a learning styles inventory and then discussing the results with the students because students may not be aware of their preferred styles of learning if asked. Because of the diverse nature of nursing students, the nurse educator may find a wide range of preferences, and this can prove to be challenging when planning learning activities because he may need to use varied teaching methods for each lesson.

13. C: According to Kolb's Learning Style Inventory, learning styles include:

- Accommodative: likes to learn through a combination of concrete experience and active experimentation, solves problems through trial and error, and tends to complete tasks
- Assimilative: likes abstract concepts and reflective observation and is more interested in abstract ideas than people and applying ideas
- Divergent: likes concrete experience and reflective observations, is imaginative with good ideas, and is emotional; likes working with people
- Convergent: likes abstract concepts and active experimentation and prefers dealing with things to people

14. A: Visual learners prefer to learn by seeing and reading, so the nurse educator should provide written directions, illustrations, and videos. Auditory learners prefer to learn by listening and talking, so she should explain a procedure while demonstrating and ask the students to repeat the steps to the procedure verbally. Kinesthetic learners prefer to learn by handling equipment and actually practicing, so she should provide hands-on experience with minimal explanation, allowing the students to explore. Most students have combined learning styles.

15. D: Scholarly integrity means that the product of student effort is created independently, so it is a violation for two students to do a take-home exam by dividing up the questions and each doing half of the work. Other violations include copying from others and posting or disseminating copies of tests, although a student advising other students about what content to focus on is generally not committing a violation. The nurse educator must ensure personal integrity as a scholar but must also monitor students so that they do the same.

16. B: The more restrictive the screening requirements, the narrower the pool of applicants. Requiring a GPA of B on prerequisite courses would probably provide the most homogeneous pool. A lottery choice from all students with a GPA of C on prerequisites would provide the most diverse pool but probably not the most competent because studies have shown that other factors, such as previous degrees or higher GPAs, correlate with success. The best choice, then, is likely the multiple-criterion screening that considers many factors with varying points awarded.

17. C: McCarthy combined Kolb's model of learning styles with the right brain/left brain to arrive at a model of four different types of learners:

- Type 1—Imaginative: Students want to understand reasons for things and prefer active involvement through listening, speaking, interacting, and brainstorming.
- Type 2—Analytic: Students want to know what to study and learn and prefer a more passive role, observing, analyzing, classifying, and theorizing.
- Type 3—Common sense: Students want to know how to apply what they have learned and prefer experimenting, manipulating, and improvising.
- Type 4—Dynamic: Students want to know about different possibilities and enjoy modifying, risk-taking, and creating something new.

18. A: William Perry's stages of cognitive and ethical development include:

- Dualism/received knowledge: Basically, there is one right solution to all problems, but at the full dualistic level, there is one right solution among wrong solutions, and people must figure out the right one.
- Multiplicity/subjective knowledge: People must learn how to find the right solutions but later realize that many problems cannot be solved, so people can come up with their own solutions.
- Relativism/procedural knowledge: At the contextual level, people understand that they must have reasons and context for solutions. At the precommitment level, they understand the need to make choices.
- Commitment/constructed knowledge: People make a commitment, explore responsibilities, and understand that it is an ongoing process.

19. B: According to the National League for Nursing, the ideal educator-student relationship is egalitarian/collaborative. Educators should consider themselves in partnership with students, helping and guiding them to learn and grow in the profession. Educators must interact with students and collaborate to establish the best methods to help them learn and to reach their learning goals. Educators must begin by assessing their own values and beliefs and must develop strategies to increase student participation in learning.

20. D: The following information must be shared with the student:

- Problem: The student must be advised of the academic concerns.
- Solution: The student must be told what actions he can take to improve grades or complete work.
- Time frame: The student should be advised of the exact period of time in which the steps to rectifying the problem must be completed.
- Consequences: The student must be advised of the action, such as dismissal, that will be taken if he cannot solve the academic problem. These general steps should be outlined in the syllabus, so all students know what to expect.

21. C: The nurse educator should refer the student to a counselor to help her deal with the stress and should not attempt to carry out the dual roles of counselor and instructor because this may result in a conflict of interest. The nurse educator has a responsibility to ensure the safety of the patients, and if a student's clinical performance is inadequate, she must be apprised of the problem, and steps should be taken to improve it. The student must be carefully supervised and observed until consistent improvement in clinical performance is documented.

22. C: The nurse educator should explain the issue to the student and ask how she would like to deal with the problem. The student might feel comfortable telling staff members and patients that she has cerebral palsy or has impaired speech, but the nurse educator cannot divulge private health information about the student. Students with disabilities are often familiar with the comments people make about them and may have surprising insight into dealing with problems that arise because of their disabilities.

23. A: The two primary issues to consider when a student with disabilities applies to the nursing program are his qualifications (disregarding the disability) and the need for accommodations to allow him to successfully complete the nursing program. If the student is qualified and accommodations can be provided, then he should receive the same consideration as other applicants. Accessibility is already covered under the Americans with Disabilities Act, so that should not be an issue.

24. D: The nurse educator cannot divulge personal information about the student to other instructors without permission, even though sharing this information may be to his benefit. The best action is to ask the student if he would consider discussing his dyslexia with other instructors and to discuss the student's concerns about doing this. Sometimes students are afraid that they will be unfairly labeled if instructors know they have a learning disability, and they may be unaware of their rights to accommodations.

25. B: The primary consideration when developing an intervention program for nursing students who are impaired because of substance abuse is ensuring confidentiality of the participants because, unless students can be assured of confidentiality, they will probably not join the program. Other considerations include outlining the responsibilities of those involved in the program as participants, counselors, faculty, and administrators and educating students about the program. The costs of the program may also be a concern, but they may be offset by the savings from student retention.

26. B: The nurse educator should advise all students about their state's licensure restrictions for those with criminal backgrounds and any appeals processes that may be available to them. Restrictions vary from state to state, but felony convictions often prevent licensure. Additionally, some agencies in which the student may gain clinical experience may require criminal background checks even if the school or state does not. Completing the requirements of a nursing program is no guarantee of licensure.

27. A: The four elements that should be congruent in curricular design are objectives, outcomes, subject matter, and learning activities. The nurse educator should evaluate how all elements fit together. The objectives and outcomes should be clearly linked to the mission and philosophy of the school of nursing and those of the college or university. Course objectives should be linked to program objectives. This internal consistency may be evaluated through the use of a curriculum matrix.

28. C: Bevis's description of curricula includes the following:

- Illegitimate curricula: taught but not evaluated, such as caring, empathy, and compassion
- Operational curricula: content such as knowledge and skills that is actually taught and evaluated
- Hidden curricula: taught unconsciously through modeling, such as values, interactions, and beliefs
- Null curricula: behaviors, skills, and content that are not taught, such as critical thinking, even though instructors may believe they are taught
- Official curricula: framework that is stated, such as on a syllabus, usually including philosophy, mission, objectives, and outcomes

29. B: Barriers to curricular change include fear of loss of autonomy and control by faculty, misunderstanding, demands for time and energy, lack of motivation, different perspectives on the need for change, complicated change procedures, vindictiveness, resentment, inadequate resources, inadequate procedures for change, lack of reward, and threats to social structure and support. Many people fear change regardless of the benefits that might be derived from it and may lack the flexibility and adaptability necessary to facilitate change unless they see a clear personal benefit.

30. A: Although all of these trends may influence nursing education and curriculum development, the aging of the population is likely to have the greatest impact because the numbers of those aged 65 and older are projected to increase by 135% by the year 2050 and those 85 and older by 350%. This will bring about increased focus on geriatric and preventive medicine as well as home healthcare and community-based medical services.

31. C: Behaviorism focuses on positive reinforcement to provide motivation to learn, with information provided by an instructor in an organized manner and facts mastered in sequential steps, with the emphasis on critical thinking and analysis. Curricula are designed to promote intellectual development, with the emphasis on science and facts. Curricula are organized according to subject matter. This has been the most common model for nursing schools, accrediting agencies, and state boards of nursing since 1950.

32. D: In the future of nursing, it is expected that most advanced-practice nurses will enter the profession with a doctorate degree and entry-level RNs will have baccalaureate degrees (BSNs). Although many current RNs have associate degrees (ASNs), there are increasing numbers of bridge programs that allow nurses with ASNs to study for BSNs while actively engaged in the nursing profession. Some states are now allowing community college programs to grant BSNs in nursing.

33. B: Because 60% of the nurses have ASNs (consistent with national averages for graduates), this provides the largest pool of potential students for the bridge program, making an ASN-to-BSN program probably the most cost-effective option. Because approximately 37% of nurses graduate with a BSN but only 20% of employed nurses have BSNs, the number of BSNs is below the national average, so the educational mobility option of a bridge program should provide a better educated staff.

34. A: Because pain is a factor in virtually all practice settings and content areas, this concept would best lend itself to integration as an initial trial. Pain control is core to nursing practice, so it can be studied in relation to different patient populations. Students may begin with studying the nature of pain and the causes and move on to assessment and treatment of acute and chronic pain. Students should gain an understanding of how pain affects patients in different specialty areas, such as cancer and orthopedics.

35. A: The student is primarily responsible for learning, and instructors must keep that in mind when some students seem to fall behind. However, all parties share some responsibility. The state board of nursing in most states establishes criteria for curriculum, and the program directors develop courses and learning experiences based on these criteria. Instructors must structure learning in such a way that the students have access to necessary information and must ensure that presentations and activities facilitate learning.

36. B: Certifying agencies currently have the most influence over master's degree programs because they provide content outlines indicating the content that the applicant for certification is expected to master in order to pass the qualifying exam. Because nursing education has become more focused on outcomes, programs have become more creative and curricula more varied, but they must ensure that students are adequately prepared for certification in their chosen specialty area and meet the clinical requirements of the certifying agency.

37. C: Orem's (1959) general theory of nursing focuses on serving patients and assisting them to provide self-care. It encompasses three theories:

- Self-care: The individual is the self-care agent, and the caregiver is the dependent-care agent. The categories of need include developmental needs, universal needs, and health needs.
- Self-care deficit: Nursing assists those who cannot manage self-care through provision of care, guiding, providing instructions, supporting, and making environmental adjustments.
- Nursing systems: Meeting patient's self-care needs may be compensatory, partly compensatory, or supportive.

38. D: The KSVME conceptual framework (Webber, 2002) includes the following components:

- K—Nursing knowledge: specific knowledge related to the field of nursing, including natural and behavioral sciences and nursing skills
- S—Nursing skills: acts/activities that demonstrate the other items in the framework (knowledge, values, meanings, and experience)
- V—Nursing values: ethical values, such as honesty and integrity, and the American Nurses Association (ANA) Code for Nurses
- M—Nursing meanings: relates to language and terms specific to nursing, such as synergy and holism
- E—Nursing experience: knowledge gained over time from experiential learning

39. C: Once an outcome has been identified, the next step is to identify the competencies, skills, and knowledge that the students will need to successfully achieve the outcome. The competencies are focused on the student and are often behavioral, in that students must demonstrate specific attributes, such as demonstrating problem-solving skills and the ability to make decisions based on analysis of information. Bloom's taxonomy (cognitive, psychomotor, and affective domains) is often used when developing competencies.

40. A: Even though the student is taking notes, listening to a lecture is primarily a type of passive learning. The instructor identifies important points and organizes the material. Many students prefer this method of learning because it is less stressful and requires little active engagement. Active learning requires active participation on the part of the student, who explores information and identifies what he or she believes are important points. Active learning may include group presentations or development of a product, such as a slide show presentation or a video.

41. D: Unstructured learning activities, such as attending a community meeting to observe activities/interactions that occur and reporting back to the class, facilitate acquisition of knowledge without specific directions from the instructor. This is also referred to as "discovery" or "inquiry-based" learning and is more commonly used in graduate-level courses than for beginning students. Structured learning activities, such as writing reports, completing worksheets, and completing reading assignments, include specific directions and/or steps that students need to follow.

42. B: Bloom's taxonomy outlines behaviors that are necessary for learning and comprises three domains: cognitive, affective, and psychomotor. In the cognitive domain, knowledge represents the lowest order of learning because it primarily involves just acquiring and recalling facts. Comprehension involves understanding new information, and application is the ability to actually apply knowledge to new situations. Analysis is the ability to break down information into component parts, whereas synthesis is the ability to take parts and put them back together in a new way. Evaluation is the ability to look at information and formulate judgments about it.

43. D: The affective domain includes five categories of feelings and values, ranked from simple to complex: receiving phenomena, responding, valuing, organizing values, and internalizing values. Storytelling is one method that is encouraged to develop the affective domain. Discussion of case studies is also frequently used to encourage students to explore their values, beliefs, and emotions and to begin to move from external control to internal. Journals and other types of writing are also of value.

44. A: According to Boyer (1990), the four types of scholarship include the following:

- Integration: includes interdisciplinary activities, such as reading extensively in other disciplines (such as bioethics, rehabilitation, and neuroscience) and mentoring junior faculty members
- Discovery: includes conducting independent research and submitting it to juried publications to share with the profession
- Teaching: includes the standard teaching roles (classroom teaching, curriculum development, and evaluation of curriculum and program)
- Application: includes various aspects of professional practice, such as consultation

45. D: Dave's taxonomy (1970) for the psychomotor domain has five levels:

- Imitation: actions include some errors and weakness in gross motor actions
- Manipulation: ability to follow written directions with some accuracy, but some variations are evident with coordination of movements
- Precision: ability to carry out an action in a logical order with a few noncritical errors, demonstrating good coordination of movements but with variable amounts of time needed
- Articulation: ability to carry out an action with good coordination in a logical sequence and in a reasonable time
- Naturalization: demonstration of automatic professional competence

46. C: Students are often reluctant to tell instructors directly when there is a problem with their presentations, even if asked, although using anonymous feedback forms after each class can provide good information. Videotaping may be of some value, but the best solution is probably to ask a trusted colleague to observe some classes and provide honest feedback. Problems might range from poor organization of information to poor presentation skills, such as speaking in a monotone voice or not allowing time for student participation or questions.

47. A: Learning constraints include the following:

- Faculty constraint: activities are inappropriate for students' abilities because of overestimation or underestimation of students' knowledge, content knowledge is inadequate, presentation skills are poor, or the educator's personal habits are distracting to students
- Student constraint: number of students, lack of prerequisite knowledge, stress anxiety, resistance, or lack of skills
- Time constraint: inadequate time for activity, questions, or feedback
- Resource constraint: inadequate facilities (classroom size or design), equipment (computers, simulators, and audiovisual equipment), or information technology (e-mail, electronic messaging)

48. D: Summative evaluations are done at the completion of a course or program to evaluate the final results, so it is appropriate to use to assess students' learning outcomes. Summative evaluations can also be used to assess the effectiveness of learning activities and teaching strategies and to determine the need for revisions to a course. Formative evaluations are those done while a course or program is in progress to assess learning activities and students' learning and to identify problems.

49. C: Bevis's (1988) six types of learning are as follows:

- Item: able to see simple relationships
- Directive: able to learn rules, safety injunctions, requirements, and exceptions
- Rational: able to use theory to make rational decisions
- Syntactic: able to gain insight by recognizing patterns and relationships
- Contextual: able to accept cultural rules, norms, rituals, and mores
- Inquiry: able to investigate, research, and theorize to develop ideas and vision

50. B: Service learning is an educational experience that actively engages students in working in the community and meeting community needs, so the activity that takes the students into the community and allows them to learn inductively about the community needs by surveying those affected by the tornado is the best example of service learning. However, students should prepare for the survey by studying about illnesses and injuries common to disasters. Service learning is more than just volunteering because it should be part of a course or program and should involve useful activities that address community needs.

51. B: One of the best ways to ensure that information is stored in the long-term memory is to link it to already-learned information, so careful sequencing of information can facilitate learning. Rehearsing, reviewing, and repeating information also help students retain information. Words associated with images are easier to recall than words alone, so providing illustrations or describing concepts that can be visualized also promotes memory. Short-term memory may last no longer than 30 seconds and is usually limited to about five to nine items.

52. C: According to Ausubel and Robinson's (1969) and Ausubel's (1978) assimilation theory of learning, the most critical factor in student learning is prior knowledge. Ausubel believed that meaningful learning was superior to rote memorization and could be attained if students study in a meaningful manner, understand the logic involved, and apply prior knowledge to learning new concepts. Ausubel suggested aids such as prompting students and providing advance organizers (comparative or expository) to help students process and learn new information.

53. D: One of the primary principles of teaching based on Knowles' model of adult learning is that the educator should plan course content and teaching strategies in collaboration with the students themselves, who should become active participants in learning and monitor their own progress. Educators must show respect for the students and help them assess their learning needs and take advantage of prior knowledge. Students should help develop learning contracts, learning strategies, and plans for evaluation.

54. B: Humanism focuses on the affective domain and affective outcomes, guiding students to more effectively develop study skills and to promote creativity. The approach is very student-centered and collaborative with an appreciation for students' individuality and feelings. Educators are expected to model appropriate and target behavior, including caring, honesty, genuineness, and respect for the self and others. Students are expected to be responsible for their own learning and carry out self-evaluations, although educators must verify competence in clinical work and mastery of content.

55. D: The nurse educator should meet with the difficult group member but should focus on how the student's behavior is affecting learning—the individual student's and the learning of the other group members. The educator should bring the annoying behavior to the student's attention, explore new behaviors, and coach the student as needed so that these types of behaviors are remedied early and do not carry over into the student's professional life. Students should be held accountable for their poor behavior so that it doesn't escalate and become a negative pattern.

56. A: The nurse educator should check administrative policies regarding violations and follow protocol. He should always be aware of any administrative policies in place regarding conduct. Policies regarding conduct violations may vary from zero-tolerance and dismissal from the program to counseling and probation. In all cases, the educator should carefully document evidence of misconduct and any contact with the student regarding the matter. If meeting with the student, it is often best to include the department chairperson. The educator must ensure that due process is followed.

57. B: The ideal size for a small group is three to five students. The nurse educator should try to ensure that the groups are heterogeneous in gender, abilities, ethnicity, and experience. Students should be prepared for group work and should understand the various roles within a group, such as leader and recorder, and they should ask to assign these roles within the groups. The educator must be sure to allow adequate time for groups to plan, meet, work, and practice.

58. D: Games are especially useful to reinforce knowledge as opposed to introducing new information. Games usually are rule-governed and may include various levels of chance but should involve the use of knowledge or skills and may include simulations. Games should be student-centered with the teacher acting as observer, but the nurse educator should lead the debriefing after the game is completed and should set guidelines. Games may be time-consuming to create and administer, and individual student progress may be difficult to evaluate.

59. C: Problem-based learning often increases the workload of the nurse educators, especially during the development phase when educators must design problems related to clinical situations. However, new exercises must be continually developed and old exercises updated, so the workload can remain high after implementation. Interdisciplinary collaboration is crucial and often time-consuming. However, problem-based learning can help students develop skills in solving problems and can encourage self-directed learning and motivation to learn. Students must be oriented to problem-based learning and given enough time to research, discuss, and arrive at conclusions.

60. B: It's clear from the results of the CAT that students feel fairly confident about preparation (locating veins, skin prep) and observation (evaluating the site) but are much less confident with practice (starting IVs with needles and catheters), with significant numbers feeling no or low confidence in their abilities. This is fairly common, but students need more practice. The nurse educator should incorporate practice starting IVs and calculating drop rates into the next lessons, but repeating the entire series is not indicated.

61. D: The nurse educator should allow for a wait time of 10 to 12 seconds after asking a question before giving a second prompt or restating the question. ESL students often need extra time to process the question and begin to formulate an answer, and some students come from cultures in which periods of silence are more common than in the United States. The nurse educator should prepare students for the types of questions that they will be asked to respond to and should discuss typical classroom dynamics, especially for international students.

62. A: Cultural awareness begins with assessment of students' perception of self and others and learning about similarities and differences among cultures. Cultural knowledge includes gaining factual knowledge about other cultures, including customs, health beliefs, practices, and family structures. Cultural understanding is recognizing that there are different values and perspectives. Cultural sensitivity is appreciating and respecting cultural values and differences. Cultural sensitivity often develops from interactions with those from different cultures, leading to improved cultural skill as the person becomes adept at communicating and performing with people from other cultures.

63. A: The nurse educator should stop assigning students to the unit. Although students need to learn that not all assignments or jobs are ideal, forcing students to deal with an openly hostile supervisor serves little purpose and likely subverts the learning processes. The students need to be able to apply knowledge learned in class in a supportive environment in which faculty and staff are caring and in which the students feel they are accepted and appreciated.

64. C: The best option is to use the dual- or multiple-assignment strategy because this allows the students to complete their required hours on schedule. In the dual-assignment strategy, two students are assigned the same patient, with one serving as leader. The leadership position is rotated daily. In the multiple-assignment strategy, three students are assigned to one patient with one providing care, the second doing research and gathering information, and the third serving as the observer, keeping a record of interactions and responses.

65. B: Psychomotor skill categorization is listed as follows:

- Fundamental: range of motion (ROM), lifting, showering, hand washing, positioning, measuring vital signs, measuring height and weight, bed making, feeding, and using body mechanics
- General therapeutic and diagnostic: inspection, palpation, percussion, auscultation, neurological assessment, administration of medications, IV therapy, isolation techniques, giving enemas and suppositories, applying heat and cold therapy and bandages, caring for wounds, catheterizing, and doing physical assessment
- Specialized therapeutic and diagnostic: suctioning, oxygen therapy, stoma therapy, eye irrigation, eye drops, nose drops, bathing infants, neonatal and child assessment, central venous pressure (CVP) measurements, doing cardiopulmonary resuscitation (CPR), intercostal catheter care, and orthopedic applications

66. C: The simulated or standardized patient is an individual trained to act in the role of a patient, and this is best used to practice skills such as history-taking and physical examinations. Simulated patients may also be used when students are learning breast exams and pelvic examinations or practicing communication skills. Simple models or mannequins are more often used for invasive procedures, such as enema practice, IV therapy practice, and CPR practice so that students don't put people at risk when they are learning and practicing procedures.

67. D: Positioning is very important. Because most of the content is coming from the screened material, the screen should be placed at the center and the educator to the side, but he should align his body so that he is facing forward, toward the audience. When speaking, the educator may turn his head toward the screen and use an arm and pointer, if necessary, to point out material on the screen, but he should keep his body facing the audience because this is the strongest position and gains the most attention.

68. A: The "two-by-six" rule is used to determine the distance a viewer should be from a projected image. For ease of viewing, the viewer should be no closer than two times the width of the screen, in this case 10 feet, and should be no further away than six times the width of the screen, or 30 feet. These rules apply to all types of projected images—overheads, videos, computer graphics, and slides.

69. B: The primary purpose of evaluation in nursing education is to facilitate learning because the evaluation can serve as a guide to help determine if teaching strategies and learning strategies have been successful or if modifications are needed. Other purposes include diagnosing problems (learning deficiencies and inadequate teaching strategies), making decisions, assigning grades, improving products (teaching modules, textbooks, and audiovisual products), judging efficiency and effectiveness, and determining the cost-effectiveness of a program or of equipment.

70. A: The first step in conducting an evaluation is to determine the purpose of the evaluation and then to establish a time frame (formative or summative) and decide when to evaluate and who will do the evaluations. The design of the evaluation is an important consideration and may involve selecting or creating an evaluation instrument. Data must be collected and interpreted with the results reported and used to make decisions. Costs of evaluation must be considered as well.

71. B: The CIPP model is most appropriate to measure the strengths and weaknesses of a program, to identify the needs of a target population, and to identify options. The acronym CIPP stands for the following:

- C = Context: identifies the target population and assesses the population's specific needs
- I = Input: evaluates the capabilities of the system
- P = Process: assesses any defects in design or implementation that may pose problems
- P = Product: assesses outcomes in relation to objectives

The CIPP model helps to determine if results are positive or negative.

72. D: The Likert scale is an attitudinal scale that is intended to evaluate attitudes toward a subject. Typically, the Likert scale comprises 10 to 15 statements that are followed by a horizontal visual analog scale, usually with five choices that range from negative to positive as follows: strongly disagree, disagree, neither agree nor disagree, agree, or strongly agree. The Likert scale may be evaluated in different ways, such as being treated as interval data (not recommended) or analyzed with the Rasch model.

73. A: When the same evaluation instrument yields completely different results with different evaluators or different groups of students, then the problem is likely with the reliability of the instrument. Types of reliability include stability reliability (reliability over time), equivalence reliability (two different forms of the instrument should obtain the same results), and internal consistency reliability (used only if the instrument is measuring only one concept). Results should be precise and predictable to some degree. Validity refers to the degree to which the instrument actually measures that which it is intended to measure.

74. A: Norm-referenced interpretation of data means that students are compared and ranked from high to low, with one student always ranked at the highest level and one student always ranked at the lowest level. With criterion-referenced interpretation of data, students are compared to present criteria to determine competency and judged against that standard rather than against each other. With ipsative interpretation of data, the students are compared to themselves over time, so this method can be used to chart students' progress.

75. C: Clinical practice can be very stressful for some students, even those who excel in the classroom or lab, so the best approach is to describe the observations and discuss them with the student to explore the reasons for the change in behavior without taking a punitive stance. In some cases, students may benefit from referral to a counselor, but that would not be the first action. The student may need additional assistance and supervision in order to gain confidence.

76. D: Although video clips may be short, the optimal length is 10–15 minutes because students' attention begins to wander after prolonged viewing, so showing shorter clips and then discussing them maintains students' interest. The educator may give a pretest to stimulate interest in the topic or other study materials prior to showing the video clips. The video presentations may be enhanced by using graphs and illustrations between video clips to stimulate discussion and to encourage a variety of points of view.

77. A: The primary disadvantage to videotaping student performance is that some students feel nervous or threatened by videotaping and may not perform at their best. Videotaping is relatively simple and takes little extra time; however, viewing the videotape and discussing it with the students is time-consuming and delays evaluation, so students don't usually get immediate feedback. Videotaping and audiotaping require the consent of the students, and the consent should explicitly outline who will view the videotapes.

78. A: Because a concept map is a visual representation of concepts and relationships, visual learners are often most adept at creating the maps. Other types of learners may find the assignment more difficult. Advantages to using concept maps are that students can demonstrate their cognitive ability with little writing and teachers can easily evaluate the students' abilities to conceptualize. A disadvantage is that the concept maps can become large and/or sloppy and difficult to interpret.

79. C: A learning contract ensures that the student is provided due process, and it is usually perceived as being less punitive than probation. A learning contract should outline the problem areas, the steps that the student must take to remedy deficiencies, and the time frame for the remediation. The learning contract should describe the obligations of the student and those of the instructor, including the steps the instructor will take to ensure that the student is competent and the consequences of failing to show adequate improvement.

80. B: The best questions for interpretive items are short answer or multiple-choice. Interpretive questions allow the nurse educator to evaluate the students' cognitive processes, and the scoring is relatively easy. The educator should ensure that the questions don't contain inadvertent clues to the answer, and the interpretive item should be relatively short and easy to read. All parts of the interpretive item and questions should be on the same page, so the student doesn't have to look back and forth between the pages.

81. D: True-false questions are the weakest, although they are very easy to grade. Students can ostensibly get 50% of the questions right just by guessing. Phrasing true-false questions can be difficult. The instructor should avoid words that may clue the answer and should avoid absolute terms (always, never), which often indicate that an item is false, or qualifiers (sometimes, usually), which often indicate that an item is true. True-false questions are most useful if, in fact, there are only two possible choices.

82. A: Standard deviation is the best measure of variability when assessing test scores. If the scores follow a normal (bell-shaped) curve, the mean, median, and mode should be the same score, with 68% of the scores falling within one standard deviation of the mean and 95% of the scores falling within two standard deviations. Mean and median are used to measure central tendency, where the mean is the average of all scores and the median is the number that divides the scores into the upper 50% and the lower 50%. The mode is the score that occurs most frequently.

83. C: In this case, "treatment" refers to curriculum and teaching strategies. Normative treatment evaluation determines whether problems with outcomes result from a failure of the curriculum or the delivery (teaching strategies). Curriculum failure can result from inadequate content, although the teaching strategies may be good. Implementation failure occurs when the content of the curriculum is adequate, but the teaching strategies used are inadequate. Theory-driven program evaluation includes evaluations of normative outcomes, normative treatment, implement environment, impact, intervening mechanism, and generalization.

84. D: The Delphi technique is designed to help groups reach consensus. A questionnaire is created by a facilitator and sent to faculty members, who then respond anonymously and return the questionnaires. The results are then evaluated, tabulated, and summarized. The results and summary are then returned to the faculty members for another round of decision-making. The rounds continue until consensus is reached. A primary advantage of the Delphi technique is that decision makers do not need to meet face to face in real time.

85. A: Focus groups are likely to provide the best qualitative evaluation of teaching strategies and teaching effectiveness. The leader should be impartial and must assure the students of anonymity and explain the purpose of the focus group and the use of the information. Internally developed evaluations provide quantitative data but often lack validity and reliability. Peer review also often lacks validity and reliability, although multiple visits by multiple peers with specific guidelines increase both measures. Self-evaluation may be biased because instructors may lack insight related to their teaching abilities.

86. D: The purpose of the 5 Million Lives Campaign (2006 to 2008) was to draw attention to the 15 million incidents of medical harm that occurred in hospitals in the United States each year and to reduce that number by 5 million over the two-year period of the campaign. The campaign has had a long-lasting influence on accrediting agencies with increased focus on preventing pressure injuries, reducing methicillin-resistant *Staphylococcus aureus* (MRSA) infections, preventing adverse effects from high-risk medications (anticoagulants, narcotics, insulin, and sedatives), reducing surgical complications, and treating heart failure and heart attack.

87. C: Hidden costs are one type of indirect cost and cannot be adequately planned for and are accounted for after the fact. Hidden costs may include faculty absenteeism and low productivity, for example. Indirect costs are those unrelated to the educational program, but they are necessary and can include heating and air-conditioning and general maintenance of equipment and facilities. Direct costs are fixed, such as salaries, or they are variable, such as dietary costs (which may vary according to census) and orientation programs (which may vary depending on staff turnover).

88. B: Cost recovery occurs when the facility provides educational services to patients and charges a fee to cover the cost of the offerings. Cost benefit usually refers to improved patient satisfaction that may result from better care or services. Cost savings most often result from more efficient or more effective care, such as when patients experience fewer complications. Cost containment includes strategies to reduce costs, such as buying less expensive supplies or changing staffing patterns.

89. A: The stages of the information-processing model of memory are listed as follows:

- Stage 1—Attention: The person must pay attention and focus on environmental stimuli, such as a lecture.
- Stage 2—Processing: The information is processed through the senses, so the person's preferred learning style is important.
- Stage 3—Memory storage: Information may be stored for up to 30 seconds in short-term memory or organized in some way (imagery, practice, or rehearsal) for indefinite storage in long-term memory. Retrieval may pose difficulties, however.
- Stage 4—Action: This refers to the person's actions or responses in relation to the information.

90. D: Role modeling is a central concept to Bandura's (1977, 2001) social learning theory, with mentoring being an example. The learner may perceive and interpret input in different ways. This theory stresses that the attitudes and behavior of the educators and staff influence the outcomes of the learners. Bandura stated that social learning is primarily an internal process with four steps: attentional phase (observing a role model), retention phase (processing information), reproduction phase (the memory is used to guide performance of the role model's actions), and motivational phase (vicarious reinforcement and punishment).

91. B: Reaction formation occurs when the student expresses or behaves the opposite of what she feels. Displacement occurs when the student acts with aggression or hostility toward others rather than directing the anger at those who are actually posing a threat. Projection occurs when the student complains that others have the undesirable characteristics that she exhibits herself. Sublimation occurs when the student converts socially unacceptable and repressed feelings into socially acceptable actions. Rationalization occurs when the student attempts to explain or excuse a threat. Denial occurs when the student refuses to acknowledge a threat.

92. C: The three determinants of learning for which the nurse educator should assess students include:

- Needs: Identify learner, select environment, collect data about and from the learner, use the healthcare team, prioritize needs, review educational resources, assess organizational demands, and consider time-management issues.
- Readiness: Consider motivating factors and barriers.
- Learning style: Assess for right brain/left brain, adult learners, Myers-Briggs, Kolb's experiential learning, multiple intelligences, and visual-auditory-kinesthetic.

93. D: The term *understand* should be avoided when writing objectives because it is unclear, not measurable, and may be misinterpreted. Other verbs to avoid include *value, appreciate, enjoy, think, feel,* and *learn.* Verbs that are recommended because their meanings are more limited include *apply, choose, compare, classify, describe, differentiate, explain, identify, list, order, recall, select, state,* and *write.* Objectives should always describe the action of the learner rather than the educator, and each objective should refer to only one action. Objectives should be reasonably attainable and specific rather than general.

94. B: The maximum number of words per slide for a slide show presentation is 25 words, and the font size should be 30 or the largest possible. The nurse educator should preview the slides from the back of the room in which they will be shown to make sure that all content is clear and readable. He should ensure that there is a high contrast between the text and the slide background, avoiding bright colors for the background. It is better to use graphical presentations rather than lists of statistics.

95. C: The nurse educator should replace the older model with a newer one to match those in use, even though this may cause some delay while she arranges to use one of the newer machines. Experienced nurses may be able to easily transfer knowledge from one piece of equipment to a similar one, but novice nurses and students who lack experience are more likely to become confused or make mistakes when trying to transfer knowledge about one piece of equipment to another.

96. C: The primary disadvantage to high-fidelity, whole-body simulators is the high cost involved in purchasing the equipment. Because cost containment can be an issue in most schools of nursing, funding may not be available. Additionally, the equipment requires a large space, and programming can be labor intensive. However, the simulators promote very good development of psychomotor skills and high-level problem-solving, and they pose little risk to the student, who can practice the same or different scenarios over and over.

97. D: One-on-one instruction is individualized for the student and requires an active learner role. If the teacher is doing role-modeling, demonstrating, or lecturing, the student is observing and listening but not taking an active role, so if she is using these teaching methods, the nurse educator must ensure that lessons are structured in such a way as to allow for student participation. For example, students may follow role-modeling with role-playing, demonstrating with return demonstrations, and lecturing with discussions.

98. B: Role-playing lends itself well to teaching affective skills because it helps students to explore feelings and to understand other people's feelings. The role of the nurse educator is to design the environment of the role-playing and debrief the students at completion of the exercise. Other teaching methods that promote affective learning can include group discussions, one-on-one instruction, games, and role-modeling, depending on how the lessons are designed. Lecture primarily teaches for the cognitive domain, simulation is for the cognitive and psychomotor domains, and demonstration is for the psychomotor domain.

99. A: When considering the purchase of instructional materials, the nurse educator must consider the delivery system (how the material is to be delivered to the students), the content, and the presentation (the form of the material). Major components of instructional materials include the following:

- Delivery system: software, hardware, projector, whiteboard, paper, posters, blackboards, TV, and audio equipment
- Content: accuracy, currency, appropriateness, and readability
- Presentation: realia (actual person and real equipment), illusionary representations (drawings, audiovisual materials, and photographs), and symbolic representations (numbers, letters, and symbols)

100. B: Although reading textbooks is the most common mode of learning, in fact, it has the lowest rate of retention, so readings should be supplemented and materials should be reviewed so students can use a variety of learning modes. Average retention rates are listed here in ascending order:

- 10%: Reading (books, pamphlets, and instructions)
- 20%: Listening (audiotapes, radios, CDs, and lectures)

- 30%: Viewing (slides, pictures, posters, and photographs)
- 50%: Listening and viewing (TV, videos, movies, and DVDs)
- 70%: Speaking and writing (teleconferencing, presenting, completing worksheets, and computer-assisted instruction [CAI])
- 90%: Speaking and doing (practice with real models or equipment)

101. B: The National Cancer Institute recommends that patient materials be written at the fifth-grade level. This is true even for college-educated patients because medical information is difficult for many people to understand, regardless of their educational background. According to national surveys, approximately 14% of adults are illiterate, 21% of adults read below the fifth-grade level, and 19% of high school graduates are unable to read. For these reasons, patient materials should be written in fairly simple language, and illustrations should be used to demonstrate concepts whenever possible.

102. C: Those with naturalist intelligence are not only skilled in recognizing elements of the environment (flora and fauna), but they also are comfortable with recognizing patterns, such as listening to and classifying heart sounds. According to Gardner's theory of multiple intelligence, there are 8.5 intelligences: bodily-kinesthetic, visual-spatial, verbal-linguistic, logical-mathematical, musical-rhythmic, interpersonal, intrapersonal, naturalist, and existential (0.5). People have different learning profiles, but current IQ tests primarily focus on logical-mathematical and verbal-linguistic, and this places students with other strengths at a disadvantage.

103. B: The nurse educator should get permission to use the material from the publisher of the book because of possible fair-use violations. Material may often be used without permission for nonprofit educational purposes, but four issues must be considered: the purpose and character of the work, the nature of the work, the amount of the work to be used, and the market effect. In this case, the chapter is in a commercial product that is essentially competing with the instructor, so fair use is not clear. There is not a specific percentage that constitutes fair use.

104. D: Video viewing is often presented asynchronously because this allows students to access the video at their own convenience. Readings are often also presented asynchronously as is submission of student work, such as papers. However, the instructor may assign a specific time to all students to discuss the videos or readings synchronously. Instructor office hours are often synchronous, with the instructor available for students to contact at specific times, whereas emails to the instructor at other times are asynchronous.

105. D: When developing simulations, psychological fidelity is especially important for the student and the educator. The simulation must be believable to the extent that the student can feel emotionally involved and feel that his or her actions have impact, either positive or negative. In real life, the educator would not want the student to "fail" with a patient, but allowing the students to take an action (or fail to take an action) resulting in adverse effects can be an excellent learning opportunity.

106. B: Although the grant covers the cost of the equipment and renovation, faculty training is especially important to reach the full potential of the equipment. Many companies now charge for training, and the costs may be quite high if all faculty members are to receive training. In that case, schools often choose to designate one or two faculty members to be trained as instructors, but setting up training courses can be time-consuming, and it can be difficult to find times when all of the faculty can meet.

107. C: The nurse educator may conclude that the difficulty level is probably too high. Generally, p values of 0.7 or 0.8, which means that 70% or 80% of students answered the item correctly, are the goal when writing test items, and 8 out of 20 questions have p values in this range. However, 9 questions out of 20 have lower p values and only 3 have higher, so the p values are skewed toward the lower end (mean p value of 0.62), usually indicating that the test questions are too difficult for the class (or poorly written).

108. A: This range indicates that the items should be revised. The point biserial index (PBI) indicates the ability of a test item to discriminate between those who received high scores and those who received low scores. A high score for an item means that students who scored high on the test tended to answer the item correctly more often than those who scored low on the test. Scores range from –1.0 to +1.0, with the higher scores indicating better discrimination. The ranges are listed as follows:

- >0.4: Excellent discrimination.
- 0.3 to 0.39: Good but could use some revision.
- 0.2 to 0.29: Marginal and needs to be improved.
- 0.2 to 0.19: Requires revision.
- to 0.09: Reject or accept multiple answers for item.
- <0.0: Reject.

109. C: The steps to the feedback process include the following:

1. Outline expectations so the students understand about the feedback process and what they are expected to do.
2. Tell students when you are beginning the process: "I'm going to give you feedback now." Feedback should be given during a procedure or immediately afterward and should be given privately.
3. Ask students to do self-evaluation, encouraging reflection.
4. Describe observations, using concrete examples.
5. Provide guidance for improving performance. This may include a written plan if necessary.

110. A: To be effective, program evaluation should be carried out on a continuous basis in keeping with continuous quality improvement. Although some organizations only do program evaluation prior to accreditation, this misses the primary reason for program evaluation—to show areas of strengths and weaknesses and to provide opportunity for change and growth. Although accreditation criteria should be included in the program evaluation, accreditation should not be the only driving force, or evaluators may overlook important aspects of the program.

111. C: Initial accreditation under the Commission for Collegiate Nursing Education (CCNE) is for a period of up to 5 years. Subsequently, programs may apply for periods up to 10 years. If a university has multiple nursing degree programs (such as BSN, MSN, and DNP), then programs may coordinate accreditation reviews by asking for early review of one or more programs but may not postpone the review. Accreditation is nongovernmental and voluntary, although it is recognized by the United States Department of Education and implies a certain degree of quality.

112. B: One of the weaknesses of the fourth-generation qualitative method of program assessment (Guba and Lincoln, 1989) is that outcomes assessment may not be adequate because of a lower emphasis on quantitative data, so evaluators must be attentive to this during the process. The primary strengths of this method are that it considers the input of multiple stakeholders and allows for considerable understanding of the strengths and weaknesses of a program.

113. D: In Chen's (1990) theory-driven program evaluation, in the implementation environment part of the evaluation, microcontext includes the effects of the immediate environment (e.g., campus housing and student services) on the program; macrocontext includes the effects of the larger environment (e.g., political, social, and economic) on the program; participant evaluates participant's (student's) characteristics, responses, roles, and demographics; implementer evaluates implementer's (teacher's) characteristics, qualifications, and effectiveness; delivery mode includes assessment of classroom and clinical practice as well as distance learning; implementing organization assesses the effects of organizational culture on the program, including faculty involvement in policymaking; interorganizational relationship assesses relationships with other agencies/organizations.

114. A: An appropriate evaluation technique for evaluating interorganizational relationships is to survey local hospitals and organizations that hire graduate nurses from the program to determine the level of satisfaction with the employees and any issues of concern. Interorganizational relationships may include formal or informal networks, cooperative ventures, collaboration, partnership, contractual relationships, and joint ventures. Issues to consider include availability of data from other organizations, community issues, characteristics of other agencies, level of involvement, organizational structures, and leadership.

115. A: Quantitative techniques for assessment of student outcomes include those forms that provide measurable data, such as written examinations, especially those that can be evaluated objectively, such as multiple-choice tests. In some cases, oral examinations may be quantitative if subjective evaluation is not part of the process. Qualitative techniques include personal checklists, rating scales, self-assessment, and observations. There is value in quantitative and qualitative techniques, although quantitative techniques are most often given more weight when assigning grades.

116. C: If many faculty members disagree with the mission and philosophy statements of the nursing program, then these statements may need revision, although it may be the case that the faculty members need more education about the mission and philosophy. These statements should be congruent with the university statements. Not including the mission and philosophy statement on the fact sheet is an oversight, but it doesn't suggest a need for revision. Students are often unaware of the specific mission and philosophy statements of a program, so the faculty should stress how the program meets its mission and philosophy.

117. D: The principle of *linear congruence* (also known as *horizontal organization)* refers to course sequencing and to the principle of moderate novelty, suggesting that entry skills and knowledge levels should be assessed so that current knowledge is assimilated before new ("novel") information is introduced. Course sequencing should involve a determination of the skills or knowledge necessary for entering students and then the sequencing of content during the program. For example, students may need to be computer literate and have a basic knowledge of math functions, including the decimal system, when they enter the program.

118. C: Clinical simulation testing (CST) probably provides the best measure of student performance. Multiple-choice exams are difficult to write well and do not adequately measure critical thinking skills. Grading of essay exams is highly subjective and doesn't demonstrate the student's ability to apply knowledge. Research papers test academic skills and information gathering but not application. CST should be uncued and interactive, with students required to make decisions based on a case scenario so they can demonstrate clinical skills and critical-thinking skills.

119. A: Generally, nursing educators are expected to have a degree higher than the program. Thus, BSN programs usually require faculty to have an MSN, and advanced-practice (MSN) programs require a DNP or terminal degree (doctorate) in the area of a related specialty (such as a Ph.D. in health policy and management). Because of the shortage of educators with DNPs (fewer than 1% of the total nurses), nursing programs are not always able to meet these expectations.

120. B: The scholarship of discovery involves the "discovery" of new information, as in research, and it is the most traditional form of acknowledged scholarship. An important tenet of discovery scholarship is that the research involved should advance the profession and provide new knowledge. Some universities stress the importance of discovery scholarship, especially related to tenure. Research needs to be conducted using rigorous standards so it can be juried and found acceptable.

121. C: The best solution is to offer to provide training classes for the other educators because this will solve two problems: it saves the nurse educator time in the long run, and it helps the other educators to become independent in programming the simulations. Because he has already spent time assisting the other educators and understands their needs, designing the classes should not be too difficult. Because he is a novice nurse educator, this is an excellent way for him to build relationships within the faculty and to demonstrate scholarship and initiative.

122. A: Health and blood pressure screenings in the community at the senior citizens' centers and retirement communities present excellent opportunities for service learning (SL) because the students are out in the community providing an actual service that may identify health problems and assist people to get the proper medical attention. Students should receive training prior to SL so they are well prepared for their roles. Reflective journals are a good tool to help students and nurse educators evaluate the learning experience.

123. D: Although all of these may provide some useful information, the best source of information about community health problems is probably the county public health department. Although services vary by state and county, programs and services may include pesticide exposure services, health alerts, sexually transmitted disease (STD) partner services, preparedness programs for disaster planning, clinical services, communicable disease units, human immunodeficiency virus/acquired immunodeficiency syndrome (HIV/AIDS) programs, tuberculosis (TB) programs, and epidemiology and surveillance. County health departments may participate in a wide range of collaborations, coalitions, and planning groups.

124. B: By making an appointment with a state legislator to discuss new proposed legislation and the impact it may have on nursing education, the nurse educator is exercising the role of advocate. Because of increasing financial constraints on nursing education and healthcare delivery, all nurses must function as advocates for patients and the profession. The nurse educator must remain informed and address safety issues and the needs of nursing education by working through appropriate channels.

125. D: The nurse educator should recognize that collaborative action is stronger than individual action and organize other nursing faculty to conduct research about enrollment trends and return on investment to present to the university administration. Complaining or attempting to apply community pressure without supporting facts may, in fact, alienate the administration and decrease the likelihood of remedying the situation. The nurse educator should try to present facts objectively and avoid expressing negative judgments about other departments.

126. B: The nurse educator should prioritize and refocus energies, with teaching responsibilities having the highest priority because of contractual obligations. She must accept the inability to agree to all requests and resist the temptation to try to do everything because the result may be that nothing is done well. Especially in the first year of teaching, she should limit committee assignments to one or the minimum required by the institution.

127. A: The activity that best demonstrates a strategy for change is proposing a committee to evaluate the need for process revision as part of an effort toward continuous quality improvement. Nursing is a dynamic field and must change constantly to meet changing information; technology; social, environmental, and social forces; and patient needs. With increased emphasis on cost-effectiveness and return on investment in healthcare, processes must be carefully scrutinized for time- and cost-saving measures and must be evaluated in relation to evidence-based research.

128. A: The Cochrane Review is one service of the Cochrane Databases and is the best resource to use to review the best evidence, positive and negative, regarding healthcare interventions. Cochrane Reviews compare data from a wide range of studies (published and unpublished) and clinical trials and synthesize the information, conducting statistical analysis. Cochrane Databases comprise the Cochrane Database of Systematic Reviews, Cochrane Methodology Register, Cochrane Central Register of Controlled Trials, Health Technology Assessment Database, and the UK National Health Service (NHS) Economic Evaluation Database.

129. C: Bias is an inherent problem with qualitative research because it is based on people's perspectives. The researcher must first evaluate his or her own biases and then determine how to best deal with the biases of others because they will distort the results of the research and impact reliability. The researcher should carefully document all decisions regarding the development of the research design (audit trail) to help eliminate as much personal bias as possible. It is best to choose unfamiliar participants, but this is not usually possible when researching a program in which the researcher is employed.

130. D: When the NCLEX pass rate falls below the target, the initial action should be to glean as much information as possible from NCLEX, beginning with group performance data, which are available free of charge and compare the group of nurses from the school to national standards. Additionally, the school can purchase curricular information. This information will show how well the students performed answering questions in different content areas so the school will know which areas of the curricula need revision.

131. B: Threat apperception, the student's assessment of threat (often induced by fear), can affect a student's ability to function, whether the threat is real or imagined. The nurse educator should help the student regain self-control and self-confidence. The best response is one that allows the student to ask for help but leaves the decision-making with the student: "What would help you feel more comfortable doing this procedure?" In some cases, a student may want more time to review or may want assistance, but the nurse educator shouldn't make assumptions about the best solution for the student.

132. C: Gender insensitivity occurs when one gender is overrepresented in a sampling, leading to the conclusion that one gender reflects the norm for both genders. In this case, although there may be more widows than widowers, male and female expressions or feelings of grief may be different, so gender is an important variable that should be accounted for. The researchers must identify the gender composition of those involved in the study and should try to have a more balanced pool of participants.

133. C: Noddings' four principles include modeling, dialogue, practice, and confirmation. Caring practice in confirmation occurs when the nurse educator encourages students to do their best and assists the students to set personal standards and meet standards of the profession. Although confirmation includes grading, it also includes planning for many opportunities to provide constructive criticism and formative feedback to students and to allow for different levels of expectations and achievement. Caring practice in confirmation encourages the use of student portfolios and self-assessment and encourages peer support.

134. D: Reflective practice means to think about the practice of teaching in order to identify strengths and weaknesses and to grow in the profession. Meeting with a group of students after class ends to discuss their learning experience is an excellent method of reflective practice because the students have had time to personally reflect about the class. Using evaluations from peers, supervisors, and students to reevaluate teaching strategies also represents reflective practice.

135. C: The curricular matrix provides a means of visualizing the course content and sequencing. It is comprised of vertical and horizontal columns. Vertical columns contain content areas, beginning with the simpler and progressing to the more complex. Horizontal columns outline the processes needed for the content, such as problem-solving and application. The curricular matrix allows faculty to easily determine what content should be taught in each course and allows the faculty to determine what content has already been covered.

136. D: The most important factor is gaining cooperation of other faculty members with the curriculum revision process is to actively include all faculty members so they do not feel that changes have been imposed upon them with no opportunity for input. Active involvement may include completing surveys and participating in standing committees and/or ad hoc committees. Faculty members should have input into the type and extent of involvement and should be encouraged to take active roles in their areas of interest.

137. B: The best approach to preparing students to pass the NCLEX exam is to provide a thorough nursing education that covers the content and skills needed for the exam. Nurse educators should avoid the temptation of teaching to the test or too heavily emphasizing the need to pass the exam because this may take valuable time away from the curriculum and increase the students' anxiety, although students may benefit from some practice taking similar tests so that they know what to expect, especially in their last year of study.

138. A: The Family Educational Rights and Privacy Act (FERPA) protects the privacy of student educational records and reports for all those institutions that receive funding through the United States Department of Education. The law covers all students age 18 and older. Parents or guardians wanting information must have written permission from the student, even though the parents or guardians may be paying the tuition. Schools can only provide "directory" assistance, such as name and dates of attendance, but they must advise the student that this information is being shared.

139. B: Academic freedom allows instructors to establish grading policies and control the teaching strategies and (to some degree) the content of their courses. However, advising students to ignore the rules of the university is inappropriate, although the nurse educator may advise the students to take legal action (such as through writing a petition) if they are opposed to the rules. Once a teacher has assigned a grade, the grade cannot be arbitrarily changed by the department or administration.

140. B: The four C's of curriculum development include:

- Compatibility: This refers to the willingness to focus attention on common needs and curriculum as a whole rather than on individual courses. The group functions as one harmonized unit.
- Commitment: This refers to the willingness to expend the necessary time, energy, and resources.
- Communication: Requirements include facilitator (to maintain focus), gatekeeper (to ensure each voice is heard and to set agendas), harmonizer (to diffuse tension), and housekeeper (to keep minutes, prepare meeting space, and monitor time).
- Contribution: Requirements include consensus, negotiation, and compromise.

141. D: The Classroom Organization and Management Program (COMP) (Evertson and Harris, 1995, 1999) focuses on rules and procedures so students can have a clear understanding of expectations and boundaries to help prevent problems:

- Rules: should be few and should outline general behavior standards and expectations of students
- Procedures: should be positively focused on activities that are required of students, such as handing in assignments, and how those activities are to be carried out; instead of negative words such as "don't" or "never," statements should use the more positive terms such as "do" and "always"

142. C: The assignment that is likely to be most effective to help a student develop emotional intelligence is assigning a reflective journal for the student to explore her feelings and emotions. The student should reflect on the clinical assignment prior to completing it and then reflect again after it is finished, discussing personal feelings and responses to the patient as well as exploring how the reality compared with anticipation of the assignment.

143. A: The SQ3R method comprises the following sequential steps:

1. Survey: Read headings, captions, introductions, and summaries and look at illustrations, photos, and other graphics.
2. Question: Ask questions about the surveyed material, such as "What do I know about this?" and "What does this mean?"
3. Read: Read carefully and note the highlighted (bolded or italicized) text.
4. Recite: Ask questions, highlight, summarize, and take notes.
5. Review: Go over the material again and ask questions.

144. D: A permissive management style is one in which the educator allows the students much autonomy but provides little guidance or classroom management, often in the belief that this results in student-centered learning. However, student-centered learning does not mean that students are left completely in control of the classroom environment because this may lead to chaos and poor self-control on the parts of the students as well as low academic skills. Nurse educators must help the students remain focused and must retain control of the environment.

145. C: Preceptorship is a clinical education model that is particularly valuable for a senior or graduate nursing student because the guidance of a preceptor, an experienced nurse in the clinical area, can help the student apply theory to practice and to have experience collaborating with other professionals. The preceptor may also serve as a role model for the student. The preceptorship is an ongoing relationship that begins before the clinical experience and continues throughout clinical practice.

146. D: The humanistic perspective on motivation suggests that motivation relates to a personal need for growth. This perspective relates to Maslow's hierarchy of needs, which includes physiological (the most basic), safety, love and belongingness, esteem, and self-actualization (the highest). From the humanistic perspective, student behavior is the result of the student's attempt to satisfy needs, beginning with those necessary for survival (food and shelter) and progressing to those that bring pleasure and accomplishment (love, freedom, power, and fun), or in Maslow's terms, self-actualization.

147. B: The committee planning for a new learning resource center must carefully consider the rules and regulations of the Occupational Safety and Health Administration (OSHA). OSHA provides many guidelines related to safety, ergonomics, hand washing, equipment, electrical hazards, hazardous materials, bloodborne pathogens, and needle and syringe disposal. If the resource center will use or generate hazardous waste materials, then the learning resource center must deal with Safety Data Sheets (SDSs), which provide information about potential hazards.

148. A: The first step to planning a learning experience is to decide on the learning outcomes, which may be behavioral or may be more general, with a focus on competencies. This is followed by creation of an anticipatory set—an environment/activity that promotes interest. Students should have active participation in materials or activities that are relevant to the student and the class. Next, the educator should select a teaching strategy, consider issues of implementation, and determine closures. The last step is to develop evaluation strategies, both formative and summative.

149. C: Kounin's theory of classroom management is that it is better to prevent problems than have to deal with them later. A central tenet is "withitness," which means that the educator makes an effort to know and understand what is going on in the classroom at all times to ensure that the students feel safe and comfortable. Accountability refers to ensuring that students are active and engaged participants in classroom activities. The ripple effect occurs when negative behavior is allowed to continue and "infects" the class, although the same can be true of positive behavior. Overlapping means multitasking.

150. D: The best first assignment is one that helps the students learn a little about each other (promoting class unity) and requires some interaction: ask students to write a brief biography to share with other students, explaining their reasons for taking the class, and ask them to comment on at least two other students' biographies. The nurse educator must use every opportunity to encourage collaboration and interaction, and she should build this into every assignment, if possible.

It's Your Moment, Let's Celebrate It!

Share your story @mometrixtestpreparation